GRASS
ROOTS

A DOWN-TO-EARTH GUIDE
TO ENJOYABLE GARDENING

GRASS ROOTS

A DOWN-TO-EARTH GUIDE
TO ENJOYABLE GARDENING

MERIDIAN

Richard Jackson with Andrew Anderson

Foreword by Alan Titchmarsh

PAVILION

First published in Great Britain in 1994 by
PAVILION BOOKS LTD
26 Upper Ground, London SE1 9PD

Text copyright © Hawkshead Ltd 1994
Line drawings copyright © Andrew Anderson 1994
Picture credits on p. 144

Designed by Grahame Dudley Associates

The moral right of the authors has been asserted.

A CIP catalogue record for this book is available
from the British Library

ISBN 1 85793 317 6

Printed and bound in Great Britain by
Butler & Tanner Ltd, Frome and London

2 4 6 8 10 9 7 5 3 1

This book may be ordered by post direct from the publisher.
Please contact the Marketing Department.
But try your bookshop first.

Frontispiece: Great Dixter is one of the
finest gardens in England.

CONTENTS

FOREWORD

When I started gardening on television in the 1980s I wanted to bring a breath of fresh air into the garden. I was tired of the sort of approach that seemed to involve earnest men in old cardigans, dibbing away in their gardens, all of which seemed to extend to at least five acres. And I always had the suspicion that there were three under-gardeners behind the scenes doing all the work, to give the impression on-screen that all of this could be achieved by anyone at home with just a little time to spare.

I decided there was another way. An approach that accepted the odd patch of weeds and occasional untidiness. 'That's our wild garden,' I would airily say, waving my hand towards a corner of the garden that hadn't received much attention lately. 'Dandelions make such delicious wine' was another line that went down very well. And I even recommended that ground elder could be a new culinary experience. I was on slightly less shaky ground when I pointed out the butterflies on the nettles, or that I had the interests of the ladybirds at heart when a neighbour noticed the rampant hordes of greenfly.

My philosophy, then as now, is that gardening must be fun. There's no point in it all taking so much effort that you don't have time to enjoy being in your garden, with enough time to sit and get pleasure from the plants. It's very easy to lose sight of the purpose of it all – and that purpose has to be pleasure.

The *Grass Roots* approach is very much one after my own heart. It's down-to-earth, it's practical; it acknowledges that you don't have to be an expert and know all the Latin names, yet you can still have just as much fun in your garden, get just as much pleasure from growing the right plants in the right places – and, as Richard says in his introduction, have enough time to sit down with a drink in your hand. Whether you've done as much gardening as I have, or whether you're a beginner with only a window box, this is a book I hope you will dip into and always find a new nugget of information or inspiration.

Alan Titchmarsh

Left: The peaceful charm of a natural pond.

INTRODUCTION

Virtually next door on the Isle of Wight are two very different gardens, which I visited for the *Grass Roots* television series. One was created by Bob and Eddie Crick. It was a neat, formal garden that was obviously colourful all year round. The scent of honeysuckle and jasmine wafted through the air and a small fountain provided the gentle murmur of moving water, a delightful finishing touch. But what was really clever about the garden was that it had been planned and planted to require only the minimum of care and attention. The brothers had achieved the ultimate in deckchair gardening — that blissful state when you can relax, have a drink and proudly watch the garden look after itself.

Just two doors away, on the same size of plot, Rachel Bradley had developed a totally different garden. It was an exuberance of planting, divided into woodland, scree and patio gardens — much more natural in character, yet needing much more hard work to care for it. Work that Rachel positively relished.

The contrast between the two gardens couldn't have been more marked, yet they had one thing in common: both were designed for pure enjoyment, and what more could you want from a garden. However, there didn't seem to be a book that showed you how to achieve this, so I decided to write one. Whether you're a keen gardener or a reluctant

volunteer, *Grass Roots* will show you how to enjoy your garden to the utmost.

If your idea of heaven is a low-maintenance garden, you'll find plenty of good practical ideas to inspire you. In the past, the concept of low-maintenance gardens conjured up visions of dull rows of solidly boring conifers and heathers. But they needn't be like that — they can be vibrant and fun, changing character with the seasons. There are plenty of superb plants which really don't need any cosseting at all; they'll grow quite happily with the minimum of attention, so forget pruning, frost protection and all those other tedious chores. Pop in some stress-free plants — I think they're worth their weight in gold. Finally, add some pots and boxes for the finishing touch. You might be surprised to know that even these can be easy to look after if you follow our planting tips.

However, if you're feeling slightly adventurous there are plenty of other ideas to tempt you. Why not have some fun and experiment with growing fruit and vegetables? This doesn't mean you've got to slave away for hours striving to produce something respectable enough to show family and friends. The key is to pick the best, most worthwhile varieties. Unless you're extremely keen, for instance, give cabbages a miss — they're far too much like hard work. And although radishes are easy, is it worth the bother if your family doesn't really like them? Concentrate instead on

Left: The white bark of *Betula jacquemontii* is beautiful all year.

something that you'll all enjoy eating, that's easy to grow and that will taste better and fresher than anything you can buy. Strawberries, for instance, which can cheerfully be grown in the ground or on the windowsill, will knock spots off the watery Spanish giants in the shops if you choose the right varieties. And even the most laid-back gardener should grow herbs. Many, like purple sage, are handsome plants in their own right, and incredibly versatile. They smother weeds, add colour to borders and are virtually drought-resistant. What's more, they taste delicious.

Hang on, you're probably saying by now, it can't be this easy – what about all the hard work that's essential to keep a garden looking good? The trick is to keep it to the absolute minimum – after all, there are far more enjoyable things to do out there. Weeds can be kept under control by a nifty combination of mulching and ground-cover plants. Pests and diseases can be minimized by growing healthy plants in the first place – and the easiest way to do this is to add a few inches of compost or manure every year. And if you take my advice and cut back on chemicals, you'll find that Nature will fight most of your battles for you anyway.

Much of this book has been based on topics shown on the *Grass Roots* television programmes. During the series a galaxy of gardening experts joined us and many of their contributions are included here. Each week we also filmed a question and answer session, and we've selected some of the most relevant questions for each chapter. My co-writer Andrew Anderson, who was the researcher for the series, has done a superb job in rewriting the rather incomprehensible transcripts. He has also written many of the Golden Rules and drawn the excellent illustrations. His contribution has been considerable and is much appreciated.

I think you'll find that this is a gardening book with a difference. It concentrates on making the most of the opportunities in your garden while leaving you plenty of free time to enjoy it to its utmost. Above all, I hope it will inspire you to experiment and try new ideas, new plants, new products. You're bound to make mistakes, but you'll have some glorious successes which will more than compensate. So whether you aspire to be the ultimate deckchair gardener or want to create your own mini-version of Kew Gardens, this book should help. Good luck, and enjoy your gardening.

Right: A colourful and well-planned mixed border.

CHAPTER ONE

MAKING THE
MOST OF YOUR GARDEN

When you peer out of your kitchen window, does the sight of your garden fill you with horror? Well, that's exactly how Radio 1 DJ Annie Nightingale felt about her garden when I visited her in Brighton last spring. To put it kindly, Nature had fought back, and won. It was a real eyesore, yet with some vigorous tidying up, the addition of simple design features like wooden trellis, and suggestions for a few essential plants that virtually look after themselves, I demonstrated how she could easily transform it into something she could enjoy all year round. Quite simply, I showed Annie how to make the most of her garden.

So don't panic – whatever the state of your garden, there are a number of simple ways of making dramatic improvements very quickly. But before you make a start, spend a little time considering just how you want to use your garden. For some it's an area for relaxing, a place for a quiet drink and perhaps a barbecue. For others it's a play zone, where kid-proof plants are going to be essential.

The next thing to consider is how much time you can spare to tend it. A pretty, colourful, all-year-round low-maintenance garden (doesn't it sound heavenly?) will take at least a couple of hours a week, while a

Left: *Santolina* 'Edward Bowles' flowering in the foreground of the yellow and pink border in the inspirational garden at Sticky Wicket.

traditional garden full of bedding plants and vegetables will require far more attention.

Once you've decided what you want from your garden, take an objective look at whether it really can fulfil all your needs. Probably the easiest way of checking is to make a list of its good points (Annie Nightingale had trouble here) and then any of the points you dislike (an ugly fence, a dismal outlook in winter).

The chances are that you're thoroughly depressed by now, so stop and cheer yourself up with a drink before embarking on the next stage.

One of the most important first steps in improving your garden is to take a dispassionate look at its layout. Sketch out the existing plot to scale on squared paper, noting which plants are worth keeping, the direction of the sun, the paths, and any major features such as sheds or trees. Then it's a matter of trying to solve the problems as simply as possible. Would the straight borders look better curved? Would a few evergreens add structure and winter interest?

Many of the possible solutions to design problems will be found in this book, and Roddy Llewellyn's analysis of cricketer David Gower's garden (see page 17) is a good example. Although David's garden is large, the design principles apply equally well to small gardens, particularly in relation to focal points. Roddy suggested that the Gowers might consider an arbour, but other less expensive features could include a tree, planted urns, or a handsome bench. These add some focus to the garden and will distract the eye from any less attractive views.

If by this time you've got any energy left and are feeling slightly ambitious, it's well worth considering adding an extra dimension to the garden in the form of a water feature. I asked Clare Bradley to explain how to construct one and she impressed me by doing it in a day – but being the Blue Peter gardener, she had probably prepared one earlier.

Over a period of months I visited a number of gardeners who had created some superb and highly individual gardens. One of the most stunning was Pam Lewis's 'Sticky Wicket', in Dorset. Pam had designed the garden in a series of concentric circles surrounding the most beautiful aromatic camomile lawn – wonderful to admire but, she admitted, needing a great deal

Right: A breathtaking view of the colour-themed borders at Sticky Wicket.

of time and effort to keep it looking good. For many people, gardening time is in short supply, so it's understandable that one of the most popular questions is always: 'Is it possible to create a really attractive low-maintenance garden?' I confidently say yes, and you can see why on pages 19–24.

Finally, one of the most essential and least understood tricks for making the most of your garden is to pamper the soil. Whether you've a brand new garden full of builders' rubble and subsoil, rather sticky clay or a light sandy soil, you can transform it by adding some

compost. Pop some on every year, use it every time you plant, and gradually the soil will improve. Not only will the plants grow better but they'll be healthier and more resistant to pests and diseases. It sounds too good to be true, doesn't it? This magic elixir is available in various forms at garden centres, but it's surprisingly simple to make your own, as Jane Down explains on page 24. And, of course, the great advantage is that it's free!

So start making the most of your garden. It really is easier than you think.

Many gardens can be transformed very simply by reshaping borders, adding focal points, hiding eyesores and, the finishing touch, clustering some plants together on the patio.

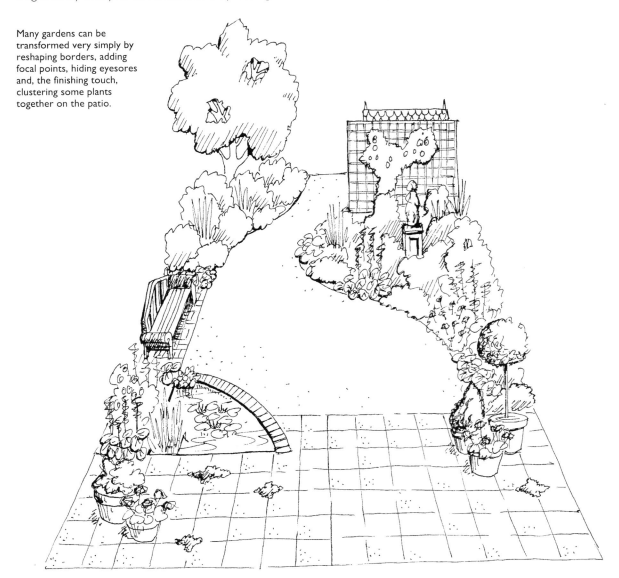

GARDEN DESIGN

'Garden design' is one of those rather grand expressions which frighten the life out of most of us, but, honestly, it's not as complicated as it seems.

Basically, it means applying a few commonsense guidelines to the layout and planting of your garden. Think about where a path will go, the shape of a flowerbed, the type of soil you have and even the aspect of the garden. You should consider these and many other points before making any plant-buying trips to the garden centre – in the long term it will save you time and money.

To demonstrate the principles of garden design, Roddy Llewellyn was invited to visit cricketer David Gower and his wife Thorunn at their new home in Hampshire. The couple had just moved into a house set in a large expanse of uninterrupted lawn and they were wondering how the garden could be given some structure and style.

RODDY LLEWELLYN:

'The thing that struck me about your garden was that it is very open. There's no intrigue, there's no mystery. It's all open and you can see the whole thing from one end to the other. What I want to do is to compartmentalize the garden by introducing hedging in the form of yew (Taxus baccata).'

DAVID GOWER:

'I think we'd like some hedging. A certain degree of intrigue but also practicality, of course. We don't want to make it impossible to get around with the mower. That's the only job I've got in this garden and I want to do it properly and easily. But I certainly think that some hedging around the pool area would be nice.'

'Swimming pools are, unfortunately, ugly objects and from the terrace it's not a pretty sight, so some camouflage is needed. I would also like to put another vista through from the sitting-room window, but this is not very popular with Thorunn.'

'I don't want you to spoil my nice terrace. You want to move the steps closer to the pair at the other end. Won't it make the terrace terribly lopsided with a pair of steps crammed into one corner?'

'We're not going to spoil it, because moving the steps over so that they are opposite the sitting-room windows is simply placing them where they should rightfully be. This will give you a great view from inside the house down an avenue of hedging. Anyway, the house is asymmetrical so it won't look odd at all.'

At this point Roddy thought it best to illustrate his ideas by laying out his design on the lawn with the aid of some plastic tape held down with some metal pins. Hedges and vistas were marked out and then everyone made their way up to an upstairs balcony.

'It's very important to look at your design from the top to get some idea of the shape. I think it looks pretty stunning.'

'Yes, it's striking stuff!'

'So you can now see where the hedging would be – around the swimming pool and the central avenue, then carrying on the same theme with yew running up alongside the tennis court, where I've got another surprise for you.'

Andrew Anderson's painting shows Roddy Llewellyn's grand design.

At the back of the house next to the vegetable garden is a tennis court enclosed by wire netting. Although it overlooks rolling countryside, this area lacks interest and so a focal point is called for.

'On this dry bank facing the tennis court I thought it would be nice to have a bench for spectators, planted up with brooms (Cytisus), and over the bench have an arbour covered in scented climbers such as jasmine, wisteria and honeysuckle. We could call it Gower's Bower!'

Design questions and answers

Can you recommend a tree I could plant for my young son that will reach an impressive growth by the time he is 21?

What a lovely idea! This is exactly what gardening is all about – planting things for the future. If you have started reading him nursery rhymes you will no doubt have come across 'Here We Go Round the Mulberry Bush'. The mulberry tree *(Morus nigra)* has heart-shaped, dark green leaves which turn yellow in autumn and would be perfect for the purpose. It's a good traditional choice and in future years you will be able to enjoy its unusual purplish-red succulent fruit.

I moved a large *Viburnum tinus* 'Eve Price' from the front garden to the back garden in February this year and it now appears to have died. What have I done wrong?

This plant is an evergreen and all evergreens are best moved in the autumn when the soil is still warm and the plant has stopped growing for the year. However, if the stem of your plant is still green, it is still alive. Cut the plant back hard near the base and this should encourage it to produce new growth.

I've just planted my garden and I've been careful to space the shrubs at the correct distance apart. Can I do anything to fill in the gaps between them while they're growing?

Make the most of the space available by adding splashes of colour with annuals such as tobacco plants in the summer and winter-flowering pansies in the autumn. Pop in some bulbs as well.

My garden is very long and narrow – how can I make it more interesting?

Try dividing it up into a number of 'rooms', or compartments, separated by hedges, large plants or trellis. Each 'room' could have a different style: the one nearest the house could have a traditional lawn, the middle one a pond and fountain, and the last could be a vegetable and fruit garden.

What could I use to cover a section of ugly breezeblock wall?

One of the best of all plants is the Boston ivy, *Parthenocissus tricuspidata* 'Veitchii'. It grows in sun or shade, is self-clinging and the beautiful apple-green summer foliage turns a stunning red and gold in the autumn.

My shed is something of an eyesore – how best can I hide it?

The simplest answer is to soften its impact by planting a large evergreen shrub like *Viburnum tinus* in front of it. Alternatively, you could put up a trellis and grow an evergreen wall shrub like pyracantha or an evergreen climber such as *Clematis armandii*.

Golden rules for design

❋ Before deciding upon a design the most important thing to consider is the budget, as this will dictate the scope of your garden. Most people spend their money on the house and have none left for the garden, so it helps to allocate money early on.

❋ If you move to a new garden, leave well alone for the first year, and take notes or photographs of what comes up. This will help you decide what you want to keep and what to dig up.

❋ Think carefully before removing any large established plants. For instance, an ancient overgrown apple tree could look very beautiful if carefully cut back – an irreplaceable treasure.

❋ In the planning stages, lay out the skeleton of a design using string and markers, rope, hosepipe or tape, then look at it from an upstairs window to get a better idea of the effect. This is the best time to make any alterations that are needed.

◉ Never be afraid to move plants, particularly if you think that they are in the wrong place or have outgrown a space – a garden is never a static place. Most plants will transplant quite happily in the autumn.

◉ The easiest time to assess the shape of the garden is in the winter. It's also the best time to decide whether more evergreens are needed for structure and winter interest.

◉ Try to keep the style of the garden in sympathy with the house. A 1930s semi with a Tudor knot garden would look rather strange, as would a cottage with a high-tech garden.

A pair of bay trees looks stylish by a formal entrance.

PLANT LIST

Plants for design: my top 10 – a totally individual and eccentric selection, but I love them.

Artemisia 'Powis Castle': Fast-growing, fine silver foliage. Thrives in the sun.

Choisya ternata 'Sundance': Bold golden foliage; needs some protection in colder areas.

Cordyline australis 'Atropurpurea' (purple form): Rich bronze sword-shaped leaves. Tender.

Elaeagnus × *ebbingei* 'Limelight': A delicious evergreen; dark green leaves with central yellow variegation.

Euonymus fortunei 'Emerald 'n' Gold': A hummock-forming variegated evergreen.

Hosta in variety: All are superb (especially 'Gold Standard'), but keep the slugs away!

Magnolia grandiflora: A wonderful evergreen wall shrub with richly scented goblet-shaped white flowers in summer.

Phormium tenax 'Dazzler': New Zealand flax. Red-variegated, arching, fan-shaped leaves. Tender.

Robinia pseudoacacia 'Frisia': False acacia. A glorious golden-leaved tree.

Salvia officinalis 'Purpurascens': Evergreen purple-leaved sage.

LOW-MAINTENANCE GARDENING

When I visited Christopher Lloyd in his glorious garden in Great Dixter last summer, he cheerfully told me that he believes in labour-intensive gardening. Somewhat jealously, I reflected on how few of us are able to indulge in that style of garden. For most of us time (and money) is limited, but we can still achieve wonderful results without hours of work. So here's the *Grass Roots* guide to low-maintenance gardening.

Beat the weeds

Unfortunately the first step towards low-maintenance gardening is the hardest, but don't let this put you off – you'll only have to do it once. You must clear the garden of perennial weeds like nettles, bindweed and the dreaded ground elder by digging them out, smothering them with black polythene or using a weedkiller.

From then on, life gets much easier and you can defeat any remaining weeds using mulches or plants. Mulches such as bark chips, well-rotted manure, mushroom compost or (best of all) your own garden compost should be applied in a 4-inch/10-cm layer on the borders in early spring. They will prevent any annual weeds from emerging, and any remaining perennial weeds that struggle through can very easily be pulled out. Top the mulch up every spring if necessary, keeping it to roughly 4 inches/10 cm in depth.

The problem with some mulches, especially chipped bark, is that they are dreadfully expensive. In less conspicuous spots you could compromise by covering the ground with black polythene disguised with a thin 1-inch/2.5-cm layer of bark. An alternative solution is to enlist the help of ground-cover plants, the harassed gardener's secret weapon. They cheerfully grow at the foot of borders, look pretty and are ruthless at smothering weeds. But beware, some of the varieties sold in garden centres are horribly invasive, so however innocent they may look, avoid *Vinca major* (the large-leaved form of periwinkle), *Lysimachia* (creeping Jenny) and the deceptively charming *Houttuynia*. Choose instead from the list on page 23.

If you're still not entirely convinced of the merits of ground-cover plants, ponder the results of the work done by one of Britain's horticultural colleges. One conventional garden took 30 hours to weed per year, whereas an identical garden planted with extra ground cover took only seven hours – a saving of 23 hours a year. Just think, you could spend all those hours enjoying the garden instead of weeding.

Picking the right plants

Some plants need cosseting but others, thank goodness, will look after themselves. Most trees, shrubs and (if you must) conifers are good news. Climbing plants should be chosen carefully, since some (wisteria, for example) need lots of work, particularly in the first few years. Overleaf, I've selected some of the best easy-care plants that virtually grow themselves. I've been a bit wary of recommending roses, but assuming that you love them as much as I do, the general rule is to pick out the newer, disease-resistant forms or the lovely old shrub roses, which are as tough as old boots.

Minimize the use of bedding plants, placing them in clumps or pots to enliven dull corners rather than planting whole beds of them. Try to avoid varieties like petunia that need constant deadheading – *Impatiens* (busy lizzies) and *Nicotiana* (tobacco plants) are far less demanding.

Canny gardeners grow herbaceous plants instead of bedding. These provide similar bold splashes of colour but are perennial, so they're far better value for money and, if you pick varieties that don't need staking, are far less demanding. Two of the best for flowers from May to September are *Diascia* 'Ruby Field' and *Scabiosa* 'Butterfly Blue', while for later colour it's hard to beat *Aster × frikartii* 'Mönch' and *Rudbeckia fulgida* 'Goldsturm'.

In case you're wondering about fruit and vegetables, first take a look at Chapter 3. Very few are suitable candidates for the low-maintenance garden, but as there's nothing quite like digging your own potatoes or picking cherries straight from the tree, you might be tempted to make some space!

Lawns

After weeding, the second most unpopular chore is reckoned to be mowing the lawn. If you've got an average-sized lawn and it's taking you longer than half an hour a week to cut it and trim the edges, then something is wrong. Perhaps you need to simplify the shape to avoid fiddly edges, or maybe you've a number of specimen plants dotted about the lawn which could be incorporated into one island bed. And is your front lawn really necessary? An area of gravel or

Plants growing in gravel make a striking alternative to a lawn.

An attractive low-maintenance garden, but a single bed around the base of the two trees would save time mowing.

paving, softened by planting, can be equally attractive.

The other point worth remembering is that every time you feed the lawn in summer, it's going to grow faster – so as long as it looks good, you could restrict the feeding to one application of fertilizer each autumn.

Watering

This doesn't have to be a chore, either. As we've learnt during the recent dry summers, established plants don't need any watering at all. Neither does the lawn – it might turn horribly brown, but it'll soon bounce back. Bedding and vegetables do need regular watering, but I've already suggested that you limit their use. Concentrate your efforts on any young plants which will need good conditions to help them establish.

One answer for easier watering could be automatic watering systems, but since they're pricey it might be best to use them specifically for pots, hanging baskets and window boxes, which are the thirstiest of the lot. A cheaper option for containers is to add water-retention crystals. These are readily available in garden centres, and I've found they can reduce time spent on watering by half. If you pop in some slow-release fertilizer at the same time, you've minimized feeding as well.

So there you are, with plenty of time in hand. That's the real joy of low-maintenance gardening; you have something that looks good all year round – from the viewpoint of your deckchair!

PLANT LISTS

Low-maintenance climbers

Choose self-clinging climbers as they don't need wires to climb on, and support themselves once they are established.

Euonymus fortunei 'Silver Queen': A prettily variegated evergreen shrub or climber.

Hedera (ivy): *H. helix* 'Goldheart' and *H. colchica* 'Paddy's Pride' ('Sulphur Heart') are particularly good.

Hydrangea petiolaris: A climbing hydrangea with mop-head white flowers. Slow to establish, then romps away.

Parthenocissus: *P. tricuspidata* 'Veitchii' (Boston ivy) is the best of the lot.

Twining climbers

Clematis, large-flowered: 'Perle d'Azur' is a superb variety with sky-blue flowers.

Clematis, species: *C. cirrhosa balearica* is a beautiful winter-flowering evergreen.

Lonicera (honeysuckle): *L. japonica* 'Halliana' is a good semi-evergreen form.

Left: Ivy is one of the easiest and most versatile of climbers.

Below: *Clematis* 'Perle d'Azur' provides a colourful display in the height of summer, when grown through shrubs or on a trellis.

Low-maintenance ground cover

Ajuga reptans 'Burgundy Glow': Evergreen carpet of plum-purple leaves. Blue summer flowers.

Alchemilla mollis: Frothy yellow-green flowers from June to August.

Euphorbia robbiae: Handsome evergreen foliage, long-lasting lime-green flowers.

Geranium 'Wargrave Pink': Pretty salmon-pink flowers all summer.

Heuchera macrantha 'Palace Purple': Splendid dark purple leaves plus dainty white flower spikes.

Hosta 'Frances Williams': Spectacularly large leaves, blue-grey with yellow edges.

Pulmonaria officinalis 'Sissinghurst White': Pretty spring flowers followed by rosettes of large white-spotted leaves.

Rosa 'Surrey': Double flowers of soft pink produced in abundance throughout summer.

Tiarella cordifolia: Foamy white flower spikes over a dense clump of maple-like leaves.

Vinca minor: Dense, spreading mats of glossy evergreen foliage.

Low-maintenance shrubs

Some need an annual prune, but it's worth the effort!

Buddleia 'Lochinch': Compact habit, soft grey foliage, scented lavender-blue flowers. Prune hard in spring.

Camellia × *Williamsii* 'Donation': The best camellia, a lovely double pink.

Ceanothus thyrsiflorus repens: A mound-forming evergreen covered with mid-blue flowers in May.

Elaeagnus × *ebbingei* 'Limelight': A stunning variegated evergreen loved by flower-arrangers.

Euonymus fortunei 'Emerald 'n' Gold': An excellent gold-variegated small shrub which turns bronzy-pink in winter.

Lavandula angustifolia 'Hidcote': The neatest and most compact lavender; trim in spring. Deep purple flowers.

Mahonia × *media* 'Charity': A superb architectural evergreen with fragrant lemon-yellow winter flowers.

Philadelphus coronarius 'Aureus': A form of mock orange with bright yellow spring foliage.

Spiraea japonica 'Golden Princess': Wonderful reddish-bronze spring foliage, turning gold.

Viburnum tinus 'Eve Price': A compact evergreen with fragrant winter flowers. Worth a place in any garden.

Viburnum tinus 'Eve Price' cheers up the winter with months of flowers.

Low-maintenance wall shrubs

Ceanothus: *C. impressus* 'Puget Blue' is the best of these evergreens.

Cotoneaster: *C. lacteus* is a handsome red-berried evergreen.

Pyracantha: 'Mohave', with orange-red berries, is disease-resistant and one of the best varieties.

Solanum crispum 'Glasnevin': The Chilean potato tree. Worth growing just for the name.

Low-maintenance questions and answers

What plants would you recommend as indispensable and indestructible for a new gardener?

Eleagnus × ebbingei 'Limelight', *Ceanothus thyrsiflorus repens*, *Ceanothus impressus* 'Puget Blue' (in milder climates) and *Rosa* 'The Fairy' are all good performers.

How can I stop the tubs and containers on the roof of my boat from drying out quickly in the summer?

Use a water-retaining gel, which is widely available from garden centres. Simply mix the gel with water, and it swells up to resemble wallpaper paste. Add this to your potting compost before planting, and it can cut down your watering by half. Also, choose plants that don't require as much water, such as geraniums, begonias and *Brachycome* (swan river daisy). This lovely little plant even tells you when it needs watering by closing up its flowers.

Golden rules for low maintenance

Consider edging the lawn with paving, or brick edging set slightly below the level of the grass, and then you can mow right to the edge. This does away with the need to trim the lawn edge.

If you're thinking of adding some new plants to the garden, be careful to avoid any that might need regular pruning, staking or spraying.

If you have a very large lawn, consider letting some areas of the grass grow longer and then develop it into an attractive meadow. This will only need mowing twice a year, in July and September.

Mass displays of bedding plants are very colourful but extremely labour-intensive. You can often improve the display and, at the same time, cut down on the number of plants required by edging the beds with dwarf evergreen shrubs, like the silvery grey-leaved *Santolina chamaecyparissus nana*. This will also help add year-round interest to the bed.

You could also dot in some shrubs to provide additional structure and height. Alternatively, add some ground-cover perennials as permanent ingredients of the bedding scheme.

MAKING GARDEN COMPOST

If you ask good gardeners the secret of their success they'll probably give a variety of reasons, but almost without exception they'll tell you how important it is to make the most of your soil.

The simplest way of improving it is to add organic matter in the form of well-rotted manure, mushroom compost or leaf-mould every year. However, by far the cheapest form of compost is the home-made variety. It really is very easy to make – if you follow the basic rules. A couple in Verwood, Dorset, had been struggling for ages to make a decent compost, so compost expert Jane Down, alias Lady Muck, went to see them.

On examining the bins and their contents closely, Jane could immediately see what was going wrong and gave them some down-to-earth advice to solve their problems.

JANE DOWN:

'First, move your compost bins, because under these trees the bins are not going to get the heat that the compost needs in order to break down.

'When you put in your garden clippings and your kitchen scraps, add over a handful of sulphate of ammonia to speed up decomposition. Do this every week, and also get your fork in there and turn the compost over to aerate it, because the bacteria that break the compost down need an awful lot of air. Keep turning it over before you add any more material to it. Don't cover the bins with plastic – use a piece of old carpet, as this will keep excessive moisture out.

'All this takes time, so don't expect perfect compost overnight. It's going to take at least six months for all this material to break down, but if you haven't got any compost after that, my name isn't Lady Muck!'

Richard's recipe for perfect compost

◦ Grass clippings – but not too many. Only about 25 per cent of your compost heap should be grass.

◦ Garden prunings – clippings or prunings are good for keeping the compost aerated. Soft prunings will break down quickly, but woody ones need shredding or cutting up small.

◦ Compost accelerator – you can buy this from a garden centre. Alternatively, use horse manure.

◦ Weeds – these help add bulk, but perennial weeds such as dandelions must have their roots removed before being added to the compost heap. As such roots take a very long time to break down, they are more likely to be reintroduced when the compost is spread on beds and borders.

◦ Kitchen scraps – vegetable or fruit peelings only. Never add cooked food or meat as this can attract rats and mice.

Simply add all these ingredients to your compost bin, cover and leave to break down. Carry on adding material in layers, until the bin is full. After a month or so, empty out the compost and fork it back in. This speeds up the process and after a few months it should be ready to use. It should have a fine, brown crumbly consistency and will contain nutrients as well as micro-organisms which will help improve the quality of the soil.

A well-made compost has a fine, brown, crumbly consistency.

You may find that you don't have enough material to fill your compost bin, but a friendly neighbour or local greengrocer may be able to help you out.

Compost and soil questions and answers

I am a keen compost-maker and have heard that comfrey plants are great to add to compost. Where can I buy plants from?

Specialist herb nurseries will have a ready supply, or try the Henry Doubleday Research Association, Ryton Gardens, Coventry, CV8 3LG. Comfrey (*Symphytum officinale*) grows quickly and its plentiful leaves have a high mineral content, making it an excellent choice for compost heaps. It can also be used for making into a liquid fertilizer. The leaves are packed into a container and then covered with water; after four to five weeks they will have rotted down to form a foul-smelling liquid resembling black tea. When diluted with water it makes an excellent liquid feed for all plants in the garden.

How can I tell what kind of soil I have in my garden and whether it is acid or alkaline?

The easiest way is to use a simple soil-testing kit available from a garden centre. Add small samples of soil to a solution in a test tube, shake it up and match the resulting coloured liquid against the chart provided. This will tell you the pH (which is a measure of acidity or alkalinity) of your soil and will give you invaluable information regarding the choice of plants you can grow. This is particularly important if you are going to grow a group of plants that need a specific soil, for example rhododendrons, which prefer an acid soil with a pH of 5.

I have just moved to a brand new house and the garden looks like a building site. Where do I start?

Concentrate on clearing the garden of all debris, making sure you dig out any rubble or bricks that have been left behind. Then try to improve the soil as much as possible by digging in plenty of organic matter or well-rotted manure. You will then have a good base on which to create your garden.

Golden rules for compost

Try to get as much air into your compost as possible by regularly turning it with a fork. This will keep the compost fresh and create ideal conditions for beneficial bacteria in the compost heap to thrive.

Compost heaps work slowly. A bin will speed up the process and make a better compost. The most efficient bin is around 1 cu. metre in size. This will be filled up pretty fast in a large garden so it may be worth having two bins – one rotting down while you're filling the other.

Unless you have a large garden, it makes better financial sense to hire a shredder rather than buying one. Why not share it with a neighbour for the day and split the cost?

Leaves can take a long time to break down, slowing the decomposition of the rest of the compost. Instead, place them in black polythene bags, add a few handfuls of grass cuttings to each bag in the spring, and the leaf-mould will be ready to use in the autumn.

PLANT LISTS

Plants for chalk

Arbutus unedo: The strawberry tree – a very choice but slow-growing evergreen.

Berberis: Any should thrive. A good variety is *B. candidula*.

Buddleia: There is a wide choice of varieties – *B. fallowiana alba* is rather special.

Ceanothus: All are lovely, but *C. impressus* 'Puget Blue' is the best.

Cotoneaster: Any of the invaluable cotoneasters should thrive.

Escallonia: 'Peach Blossom' is a superb variety.

Hedera (ivy): Look out for *H. helix* 'Goldheart' and *H. colchica* 'Paddy's Pride' ('Sulphur Heart').

Philadelphus: Mock orange. 'Manteau d'Hermine' is particularly good.

Weigela: Pink-flowered *W. florida* 'Variegata' is very pretty.

Plants for light sandy soil

Berberis: All varieties are as tough as old boots.

Cistus (rock rose): Slightly tender. I love the variety 'Silver Pink'.

Cytisus (broom): One of the best is *C. × praecox* 'Allgold'.

Elaeagnus: Look out for *E. × ebbingei* 'Limelight'.

Hibiscus (tree hollyhock): *H. syriacus* 'Dorothy Crane' is rather good.

Lavandula: Any, but *L. angustifolia* 'Hidcote' and 'Twickel Purple' are recommended.

Potentilla: Any. *P. fruticosa* 'Primrose Beauty' is very pretty.

Rosmarinus (rosemary): An excellent hedging plant.

Senecio: Good grey-leaved shrubs.

Spiraea: *S. japonica* 'Golden Princess' is particularly good.

Plants for heavy clay

Abelia: Good late summer flowers.

Berberis: Any; an amazingly adaptable plant.

Chaenomeles (Japanese quince): *C. speciosa* 'Moerloosei' is wonderful – despite the name!

Cornus (dogwood): The red-stemmed, variegated *C. alba* 'Elegantissima' is the most elegant.

Philadelphus (mock orange): *P.* 'Manteau d'Hermine' is the neatest.

Rosa (rose): They will all revel in clay.

Spiraea: Will grow virtually anywhere.

Viburnum: So will these – what a great family of shrubs.

MAKING A POND

One of the most satisfying and enjoyable garden features is a pond. There's nothing quite like sitting back on a warm summer's day listening to the sound of the water and watching the antics of frogs, pond skaters and (if you're lucky) dragonflies. Ponds are a magnet for wildlife and provide endless free fun.

Clare Bradley, the Blue Peter gardener, showed me how to build a formal pond in a small town garden in Romsey, Hampshire. With her was Charlie Dimmock, manager of the local water garden centre.

With careful planning and lots of hard work, Clare Bradley and Charlie Dimmock built this pond in a day. Most of us would need a whole weekend!

The size and style of the garden dictated that the pond should be formal and would be positioned close to the house where it could be seen all year round. A design was chosen incorporating railway sleepers for edging and an urn dug up in the garden as a waterfall. The area was cleared and the shape marked out with a hosepipe. Then it was up with the sleeves and down to the digging. The first level to dig to was the marginal shelf where plants that like shallow water would grow. Then, moving to the centre of the pond, Clare and Charlie dug down to the deepest point.

CLARE BRADLEY

'So what depth are we at now, then?'

CHARLIE DIMMOCK

'We're at 27 inches [70 cm]. We want 24 inches [60 cm] of water, which will keep the fish happy in winter, so that's given us 3 inches [7.5 cm] to allow for the sand and for the water level to be a bit lower than the top.'

'What about the top edge of the pond? It looks almost level to me but it's crucial to get it absolutely right, isn't it?'

'That's right, because as soon as you put water into the pond it will find the level. So if the edge is higher at one corner than the other you'll get a big gap between the pond edge and the water level which looks terrible, and the liner will show. Always check the levels with a spirit level and a plank, not forgetting to check diagonally across the pond as well. Once that's done all we have to do is measure up for a liner. This pond has straight sides so it's just a straightforward measurement.'

'

Take time to check that the levels are accurate.

You mentioned a formula. What's that for?'

'That's if you had an irregular-shaped pond with sloping sides. All ponds, unless they are made out of something like concrete, should have slightly sloping sides, otherwise they can erode. To calculate the size of liner you will need, measure your maximum length and maximum width. Then measure the depth of the pond (at its deepest point), double it and add it to the measurement of the length and the width.

'So, say that your pond was 10 ft [3 m] long by 5 ft [1.5 m] wide and 2 ft [60 cm] deep. You double the depth, so that makes 4 ft [1.2 m]. Add this to the 10 ft [3 m], making 14 ft [4.2 m], and to the 5 ft [1.5 m], making 9 ft [2.7 m], and you know that you need a liner 14 ft × 9 ft [4.2 × 2.7 m]. This will also give you an overlap of 6 inches [15 cm] all round.'

'I think I got all that. We've just dug all the soil out – now we're putting something back in, but the sand is very important, isn't it?'

'Yes, with both liners and fibreglass ponds you want to stop any stones coming through. The sand acts as a cushion and if you have to stand in the pond then the liner won't be pierced by any stones.'

Adding sand cushions the liner and prevents stones from piercing it.

The liner was then loosely laid into the hole and the hosepipe was turned on. As the pond filled with water the liner took on the shape of the pond, moulding itself to the different levels and shelves. Clare and Charlie used a butyl liner with a 20-year guarantee. Using cheap alternatives, such as builders' plastic, is not recommended as they never last very long. Other PVC liners have five- and ten-year guarantees and, provided you take time putting them in and put down

a layer of sand, they should last for a reasonable amount of time.

Once the pond is filled with water trim off any excess liner, leaving at least 6 inches/15 cm. This can be hidden under various forms of edging, depending on the style of the pond. Informal or wildlife ponds can have turf right up to the water's edge, or even a boggy area planted with moisture-loving plants. Formal ponds require a smarter finish and many materials such

This cross-section illustrates the different planting levels, including a marginal shelf for plants that like to grow in shallow water. On the right is a shallow boggy area where moisture-loving plants thrive.

as brick, paving and wooden decking would be suitable. Charlie decided that recycled railway sleepers fitted in well with this small town garden.

If you are considering adding moving water in the form of either a fountain or waterfall, this is the point at which you should sort out the electrics. Unless you are lucky enough to have a stream running through your garden, you will have to use an electric pump to recycle your pond water. This will require a weatherproof electrical supply near to the pond. If you are in any doubt as to how to go about installing a pump it is wise to call in a qualified electrician, as water and electricity can be a lethal combination.

Once the pond is finished, leave it for a week or so before adding any aquatic plants. Allow the plants to settle in for a few weeks and root well before adding any fish, as a tug from a hungry mouth can uproot a newly planted specimen.

In Charlie and Clare's pond, variegated iris (Iris laevigata 'Variegata'), harlequin plant (Houttuynia cordata), Canadian pondweed (Elodea canadensis) and a water lily (Nymphaea 'James Brydon') finished the design.

Charlie fixes the sleepers into position. Be very careful if using hammer and nails near pond liners!

The pretty blue flowers of *Iris laevigata* gracing the edge of a pond.

Golden rules for ponds

Try to buy the best liner you can afford – you pay for what you get and short cuts like plastic will last nowhere near as long. Line the hole first with a layer of sand or old carpet. Never use newspaper as it rots down and causes gases to build up underneath the liner.

Always site your pond in as open and sunny a position as possible. Don't put it under overhanging trees or next to a weeping willow where the leaves will fall in during autumn and rot down, causing harmful toxic gases to build up.

Choose your aquatic plants carefully. Aim to get a balance between the pond size and the number of plants, and choose water lilies with great care. Many are quite rampant, so check your facts or ask a specialist nursery.

Be patient. Plants and fish take time to settle in so your pond may start off murky. Don't use chemicals to clear it — just wait for the plants to establish. It may take a couple of seasons, but your pond will clear.

Pond questions and answers

Do I have to have a water pump in my pond for the water to be clear?

The simple answer is no. As long as you get the balance right between the number of plants and the water surface area, your pond should remain perfectly clear. However, a pump will help to oxygenate the water and can be particularly useful when 'the weather is stormy, causing fish to gulp for air. This can be simply remedied by adding a fountain or waterfall which keeps the water moving, thereby providing a constant supply of oxygen-rich water.

I have recently made a large wildlife pond which is quite well stocked with plants but is now being taken over by blanket weed. How can I get rid of it without using chemicals?

As your pond is relatively young, the plants are not yet established enough to create a good balance. Too much light getting into the water encourages algae and blanket weed to develop. Once plants such as water lilies have established they will cut down the light entering the water, and so reduce the blanket weed. Until then simply use a cane and remove the weed by hand. Adding bundles of straw to the pond will help, because as the straw decomposes it uses up nitrogen that the blanket weed needs, so stopping it from developing.

A heron recently cleaned out all the fish in my pond. How can I deter it from calling again?

Herons can be a problem, especially as they will visit a pond in the early hours of the morning when you're not around to scare them away. Herons always have to step into a pond to fish, so place black thread around the edges on canes or plant the pond edges thickly, and it should deter them. For drastic measures, use a heron scarer which is activated by a tripwire and emits a loud bang.

PLANT LIST

Best pond plants

Acorus gramineus 'Variegatus': Variegated evergreen rush, forming neat tussocks at pool edges.

Aponogeton distachyos: Water hawthorn, unusual sweet-scented white flowers.

Calla palustris: Glossy dark green leaves, white arum-like flowers.

Caltha palustris 'Flore Pleno': Double form of marsh marigold, ideal for shallow water.

Carex elata 'Aurea': Superb golden sedge for pool edges. Divide every two years.

Iris laevigata: Best of all the water irises. Bright blue flowers with gold markings.

Menyanthes trifoliata: Bog bean. Extraordinary fringed white flowers.

Myosotis scorpioïdes: Water forget-me-not. Long-flowering and vigorous but easy to thin out.

Nymphaea 'Laydekeri' in variety: Free-flowering, compact water lilies.

Orontium aquaticum: Waxy leaves, yellow-tipped white 'flower' spikes in May.

CHAPTER TWO

THE ORNAMENTAL GARDEN

When I started my gardening career, one of my greatest experiences was helping to stage Hillier's gold medal-winning plant displays at the Chelsea Flower Show. The first, and most time-consuming, job was positioning the 20 ft/6 m high trees. The show manager, a wonderful man called Martin Drew, had us shuffling them to and fro until he was quite certain that they were in just the right spot. I once asked him why he was so particular, and he replied that if you get the structure and height right, the rest is easy – and it always was. The shrubs were slotted in, providing striking foliage contrasts, followed by roses and herbaceous plants for the final splashes of colour. The displays always looked superb, and when I told Martin so, he grinned and said, 'Use the same principles for any garden you make and you won't go far wrong.'

That was one of the best pieces of gardening advice I've ever been given. Take plenty of time in deciding where the larger structural plants like trees are going to grow. I wander around the garden with a bamboo cane, plunge it into a likely spot and rush back to the bedroom window to see if it looks as if it's in the right position. All of this feverish activity provides a great source of amusement for my next-door neighbours,

Left: A lovely group of the white-barked *Betula jacquemontii* makes a striking focal point in a subtly planted border.

but it's still the best way I know of placing trees in the garden.

Incidentally, don't be put off planting a tree because you think they all grow to enormous heights. While some do, there are plenty of superb smaller varieties which will eventually grow to heights ranging from only 6 ft/1.8 m to 25 ft/7.6 m. It's also worth considering what shape would be best – a weeping tree might be perfect for a space in the lawn, while a narrow upright variety could look marvellous in a border. Try to select one that provides more than one season of interest. Crab apples (*Malus*), with their bonus of autumn fruits, are far better value than flowering cherries (and if you need any more persuading, you can make the most delicious jelly from the fruit). One of my own favourite trees is a tall-growing birch, *Betula jacquemontii*, which has stunning white bark that can be enjoyed all year around. You've probably already guessed that I'm pretty keen on trees – they add height, structure and a wonderful sense of permanence to a garden.

When it comes to choosing shrubs, be a bit wary. There's a bewildering choice at garden centres, but rather than picking up the nearest with pretty flowers (I know it's tempting, but steel yourself), try to be selective. Choose varieties that will meet a particular need. If your garden looks dull in winter, look out for an evergreen like *Viburnum tinus* 'Eve Price', which is a cracker, and as tough as a night-club bouncer. Alternatively, camellias are among the finest of all evergreens – and they're surprisingly easy to grow if you follow Jennifer Trehane's hints on page 35.

One of Martin's other little tricks was to create distinct areas using a backcloth of climbing plants. Climbers are an invaluable source of colour but, again, choose with care. Some are far too vigorous (the appalling Russian vine, *Polygonum baldschuanicum*, should be avoided like the plague), so go for sociable climbers like Boston ivy (*Parthenocissus tricuspidata* 'Veitchii'). Make the most of scented climbers like honeysuckle and jasmine by placing them near doors and windows. For smaller spaces, one of the finest plants would be a clematis, rightly termed the 'queen of climbers'. A large-flowered variety would be better than some of the more rampant species. Anne Swithinbank discovers more about them on page 38 from expert Raymond Evison.

Since I worked at Hillier's there's been a revolution in roses. Hybrid teas and floribundas have had a reputation for being difficult to grow, but breeders are successfully introducing a whole range of varieties that are far more disease-resistant as well as being suitably compact for the smaller garden.

Some gardeners wouldn't dream of giving a modern rose any space at all, however compact it might be; for them, the old shrub roses reign supreme. Part of the undoubted charm of these is that they associate so well with other plants, as Penelope Hobhouse noted when she toured that Mecca of old roses, Mottisfont Abbey (page 39).

While modern roses may be out of favour with some, herbaceous perennials are definitely in with everybody. If you want to create great swathes of colour quickly and cheaply, these are the plants to go for. They're ideal for mixed borders and many can be enjoyed for months on end, the plants growing bigger and better every year. One of the country's most influential gardeners, Christopher Lloyd, relishes the challenge of creating exciting plant associations with herbaceous plants in particular, as he explains to gardening author Graham Rice on page 42. I'm rather keen on using herbaceous plants as a final boost to the late summer garden and you'll find my favourite varieties on page 44, inspired by my visit to Michelham Priory.

Thinking back, the one element missing from Martin Drew's glorious displays was bedding plants because at the time they weren't considered suitable for an elegant Chelsea garden. How things have changed in the past few years! Plant breeders may be criticized for producing a red delphinium, but their progress with bedding plants is a triumph. The humble *Impatiens* (busy Lizzie) has been transformed into one of the finest of all bedding plants, and the winter-flowering pansy is one of the new wonders of the world. But we can still improve the displays in our gardens, as Graham Rice explains on page 46.

Martin's Chelsea garden used to take four days to build. Yours may take a little longer, but by following the tips in this chapter you too could have a superb ornamental garden. And if it wins a gold medal, do let me know – perhaps I could pop round and plant a commemorative tree!

TREES AND SHRUBS

Camellias feature less in our gardens than they deserve because they suffer from a common misapprehension: many people are frightened of planting them because they look so exotic and fragile when they flower, yet these hardy evergreens are among the best of all garden plants and are remarkably tough. I visited one of the world experts, Jennifer Trehane, at her nursery in Dorset to ask her the secrets of success.

JENNIFER TREHANE:

'Camellias thrive in a sheltered spot in semi-shade and prefer an acid soil. They are perfect to grow against a wall and make an excellent choice for containers where, if regularly fed and watered, they will produce rose-like flowers in many forms, ranging from singles to the more popular doubles and peony-forms.

'If you want lots of flowers, watering is absolutely vital, particularly if your plants are growing in containers. Lack of water when the buds are forming, between July and the end of September, will very often lead to flower buds dropping off. This very common problem is disappointing, but it can be easily remedied by mulching thickly around the base of the plant with organic matter, leaf-mould or even lawn clippings to lock water into the ground. Camellias in containers need regular watering during this crucial time to help flowers form for next year.

'Feeding is the other important thing. Use a granular feed specially formulated for acid-loving plants like azaleas, rhododendrons and camellias. Only feed during the growing season, never in the winter, as the plants cannot absorb fertilizer in the cold winter months. Sprinkle it around the base of the camellia in April, after flowering, and then give another dose at the beginning of July when the plant is really starting to grow. This should see it through the winter.'

PLANT LIST

Best shrubs (and one conifer!)

Aucuba japonica 'Crotonifolia': A laurel for all soils and situations. The leaves are heavily spotted with gold.

Choisya ternata: A neatly rounded evergreen with orange-scented leaves and flowers. 'Sundance' is a golden form.

Cornus alba 'Elegantissima': Grey-green leaves heavily edged with white; shining red stems in winter.

Erysimum 'Bowles' Mauve': A shrubby perennial wallflower with attractive mauve flowers almost all year.

Ligustrum ovalifolium 'Aureum': A golden-variegated form of the humble privet. A good specimen shrub.

Mahonia japonica: A strikingly architectural evergreen with long sprays of pale yellow winter flowers.

Photinia × *fraseri* 'Red Robin': Dark glossy leaves, fiery red young growths in spring.

Thuja occidentalis 'Rheingold': A cone-shaped dwarf conifer with bright gold leaves turning bronzy in winter.

Viburnum tinus 'Eve Price': A compact, glossy evergreen with clusters of scented white flowers in winter.

The unusual cinnamon-brown peeling bark of *Acer griseum*, one of the finest of all garden trees.

PLANT LIST

Best trees (with ultimate height and spread)

Acer griseum (paperbark maple): Mahogany peeling bark and superb autumn colour. Slow to establish. 30 × 10 ft/9 × 3 m.

Amelanchier lamarckii (snowy mespilus): Spring flowers, summer fruits and lovely autumn colour. 22 × 21 ft/6.6 × 6.5 m.

Betula pendula 'Tristis': A beautiful weeping form of the silver birch. 65 × 26 ft/20 × 8 m.

Malus 'Golden Hornet' (crab apple): A heavy autumn crop of shining golden fruits which persist well into winter. 23 × 17 ft/7 × 5.2 m.

Malus 'John Downie' (crab apple): Upright growth, large orange-red fruits. 23 × 17 ft/7 × 5.2 m.

Prunus serrula: Magnificent bark, shining coppery red in peeling layers. 39 × 30 ft/12 × 9 m.

Prunus × *subhirtella* 'Autumnalis': Flushes of semi-double white flowers in the depths of winter. 24 × 18 ft/7.2 × 5.4 m.

Pyrus salicifolia 'Pendula': Weeping silver-leaved pear. 30 × 26 ft/9 × 8 m.

Robinia pseudoacacia 'Frisia': A glorious golden tree, very lush. Avoid exposed sites. 36 × 18 ft/11 × 5.5 m.

Sorbus aucuparia 'Sheerwater Seedling': A fast-growing upright form of mountain ash with orange-red fruits. 33 × 18 ft/10 × 5.5 m.

Trees and shrubs questions and answers

The camellia bush in my garden is looking very sick. Can you tell me what is wrong with it?

Your plant is suffering from a variety of problems. The first is a sticky substance called honeydew all over the leaves. This is secreted from insects such as aphids, greenfly and scale, which are either on the plant or on overhanging trees. While honeydew doesn't directly harm the plant, the black mould (sooty mould) which will then grow on it can cause damage; it cuts down the light entering the leaf, stopping it from making food and so weakening the plant. The best way to get rid of both honeydew and mould is to clean them off by hand with soapy water. There are also signs of scale insect, a small brown scale-like pest that lives on the underside of the leaf. It is very difficult to get rid of, so it is best to use a suitable insecticide, making sure you spray under the leaves. The browning of the leaf tips and edges means that the plant is suffering from stress, caused in this case by insect damage. Sort out the pests and pamper the plant with regular watering, mulching and feeding with Miracid. This should all help to put it right.

When and how should I plant a shrub?

Generally, all container-grown plants can be planted at any time when the soil is not frozen, waterlogged or bone dry. For most hardy plants autumn is the very best time, allowing them to establish a good root system during the winter. Planting at other times of the year is fine as long as you take extra care in watering regularly.

Dig a hole twice the width of the pot, fork over the bottom of the hole then mix a generous amount of garden (or bought) compost with the excavated soil. Fill in a little, then place the shrub in the hole to check that the top of the soil in the container will be at ground level. Ease the plant out of the pot, place in the hole and add the compost mix, firming it down as you go. Leave a slight dip in the soil to help collect water, and water in well. Mulch with bark chippings, compost or a sheet of black polythene disguised with a layer of soil.

Golden rules for trees and shrubs

As a rough guide for the safe planting of a tree near the house, check its ultimate growing height and plant it at that distance from the house if you have an older property, or three-quarters of the ultimate height if the house is modern (post 1950).

To choose the best tree for your garden, why not visit an arboretum or botanic garden? One of the best arboreta is Hillier's, near Romsey in Hampshire. You'll find a wonderful selection of trees grown to mature perfection.

The slow-growing ornamental Japanese maples are inordinately expensive, so protect your investment by planting in partial shade, out of strong winds. Keep them well mulched to prevent drying out.

Variegated trees and shrubs occasionally produce green-leaved shoots. These are much more vigorous than the variegated shoots and can eventually take over, so prune them right out as soon as you spot them.

To liven up a dull corner of the garden, consider planting a yellow-leaved shrub such as *Philadelphus coronarius* 'Aureus'. This adds instant sunshine all spring and summer. For winter impact, try *Elaeagnus × ebbingei* 'Limelight'.

Malus 'Golden Hornet' in its autumn glory, laden with yellow berries.

CLEMATIS AND ROSES

The clematis is one of the most popular and reliable of all climbing plants. Pamper them in their first year (plant deep, give lashings of food and water) and you'll have an abundance of gorgeous flowers for many a long year. They're good companions, too, mixing beautifully with other lovely climbers such as roses. Gardening writer Anne Swithinbank visited Raymond Evison at his clematis nursery in Guernsey to learn a little more about this glorious family of plants.

ANNE SWITHINBANK:
'What sort of clematis would you recommend an amateur gardener to start with?'

RAYMOND EVISON:
'The perfect beginner's clematis would be one called 'Elsa Spath'. It grows well and produces large mid-purple flowers all through the growing season. The flowers can fade in sunlight, but it's a really good choice.'

'Why are you so fond of the small-flowered varieties?'

'I think they are a fascinating group, with their small nodding flowers. Some of them are even scented. Their great advantage is that they usually have a longer flowering period but, even more importantly, they don't succumb to the dreaded clematis wilt. One of my favourites is called Clematis viticella 'Mme Julia Correvon'. This will grow to a height of 15 ft [4.5 m] and produces masses of small red flowers from mid to late summer. It would look equally good planted through a climbing rose or a garden shrub.'

'So how would you go about planting a clematis?'

'Late spring or early summer is the ideal time. Choose a healthy plant growing up a support, and check that it is firmly rooted and producing new shoots. Prepare a hole about 18 inches [45 cm] across and the same in depth, and mix in some organic matter. Plant the clematis 2 inches [5 cm] deeper than its original soil level. This helps it get established, keeps it moist and, most importantly, reduces the risk of clematis wilt. If the plant gets this disease it could still recover and throw up new shoots.'

'And what about pruning?'

'Well, it's very simple; if you remember the rhyme "If your clematis flowers before June, don't prune", you can't go wrong.'

For those who need to know what to do about varieties which flower after June, it's worth passing on one of Percy Thrower's tips: cut any large-flowered clematis down to 12 inches/30 cm every February.

One of Raymond Evison's favourite varieties, *Clematis viticella* 'Madame Julia Correvon'.

Roses

However fond you are of them, you'll probably admit that most roses are actually quite ugly when they're not in flower. The traditional hybrid tea rose bed must be one of the most dismal sights in the garden for the eight months of the year when there are no blooms to distract from the gaunt stems. The solution is to grow roses with other plants. The traditional rose bed, for instance, could be edged with lavender and you could add some pretty ground-cover plants.

Within the walls of the old kitchen garden at Mottisfont Abbey is a superb collection of roses cleverly combined with other plants. Gardening writer Penelope Hobhouse visited it and discussed some particularly eye-catching plant combinations with the head gardener, David Stone.

DAVID STONE:

'Most of the roses we grow are the old-fashioned varieties, which form rather loose, rounded bushes, particularly when they're bowed down under the weight of the blooms. So we plant upright plants between them to form vertical lines as a contrast. For example, we grow white foxgloves in great profusion under the climbing Alba rose.'

PENELOPE HOBHOUSE:

I think it's very successful. The creamy-white of the foxgloves goes so well with the beautiful flowerheads of the rose.'

'You get such wonderful value with a rose like Alba – beautiful foliage, lovely flowers in mid-summer, and as soon as the flowers are over they start developing those wonderful orange hips, which will last into late autumn.

'Whatever you plant with your roses, it doesn't have to be rare or unusual. The best effects can be achieved using the simplest of plants – like catmint (Nepeta × faassenii), cranesbill (hardy geranium) and sisyrinchium. All of these have lovely texture and colour, and contrast well with roses.'

'A wonderful way to grow climbing roses is up through a fruit tree.'

'At Mottisfont we grow Rosa gallica 'Complicata' and a clematis through a pear tree.'

'So you have a succession of flowers, starting with the pear blossom, then the rose, and then the wonderful dark, velvety Clematis 'Jackmanii'.

A beautiful example of companion planting: *Rosa* 'Madame Isaac Pereire' growing with catmint (*Nepeta × faassenii*).

PLANT LISTS

Best climbing roses

As nominated by members of the Royal National Rose Society.

'Albertine': A large, coppery pink rambler, strongly scented, almost double blooms. Flowers once.

'Compassion': Well-shaped orange/apricot flowers, tinted salmon pink, and a sweet fragrance.

'Golden Showers': Large semi-double blooms of golden yellow fading to cream. Good fragrance. Good for a north wall.

'Handel': Small semi-double flowers of creamy blush edged with pink.

Rosa 'Albertine' is glorious, but flowers only once a year.

'New Dawn': Silvery blush-pink flowers with a fresh, fruity fragrance.

Best hybrid teas (large-flowered)

'Elina' (formerly 'Peaudouce'): Delicately refined flowers of pale primrose yellow. A classic.

'Just Joey': Coppery orange, free and continuous flowering. A good cut flower.

'Fragrant Cloud': Exceptionally fragrant coral-coloured flowers.

'Peace': Light yellow, tinged pink. Large, heavy blooms.

'Silver Jubilee': Perfectly formed pink flowers shaded apricot, peach and cream. Fragrant.

Rosa 'Peace' – many people's favourite hybrid tea rose.

Best floribundas (cluster-flowered)

'Anisley Dickson': Lightly fragrant double flowers of soft salmon pink.

'Anne Harkness': Large sprays of saffron orange – an excellent cut flower.

'Iceberg': Pure white double flowers. Prolific, often flowering into winter.

'Korresia': A particularly attractive shade of yellow with good fragrance and disease resistance.

'Sexy Rexy': An awful name but lovely camellia-like pink double flowers.

Best old shrub roses

'Celestial': Small buds opening to semi-double shell-pink flowers, sweetly scented.

'Fantin-Latour': Beautifully formed ruffled flowers, blush pink with a delicate fragrance.

'Madame Hardy': A beautiful cupped white double. Perfect form, subtle lemony fragrance.

'Madame Isaac Pereire': Huge cupped crimson flowers with a rich fragrance.

Golden rules for clematis and roses

If pruning a rose fills you with dread, choose a rugosa – the only pruning they need is when they get too big. They will reward you with simple scented flowers and colourful hips in autumn.

Consult your books carefully so that you will be able to choose varieties that flower one after another to guarantee colour from early spring right through to late autumn.

Be adventurous with clematis and experiment with growing them through lots of different plants. They could brighten up an old tree or even sprawl through a bed of heathers.

If you are growing your clematis on a support, make sure it is firmly fixed to the wall. A clematis like *montana* can become a large, heavy plant and could easily pull down a poorly secured trellis.

Trials by the Royal National Rose Society and *Gardening Which?* have proved that pruning hybrid tea and floribunda roses doesn't have to be as complicated as we all thought. Amazingly, they've found that traditional pruning is unnecessary – you will get excellent growth and a mass of blooms on strong plants by cutting straight across the whole bush with secateurs or even a hedgetrimmer. Don't worry about cutting to a bud – the stem will naturally die back to a strong shoot.

Clematis and rose questions and answers

Can you tell me how I should prune my climbing rose?

The idea is to encourage the strong climbing shoots to produce as many laterals (side shoots) as possible, as it will be these that produce the flowers. In the first few years train the leading shoots in lots of different directions, bending them around trellis or poles or, if against a wall, bend the branches down so that they are horizontal and fix them to wires. The side shoots they then produce should be pruned to about a third of their length every year. Ideally you should do this in the autumn, after flowering.

My rose bush is growing very well but is not producing any flowers. Why?

It sounds as though you are treating your rose too well. Next year restrict the feeding to a high potash feed, which will encourage flowers. Don't forget to prune your plant in March and check to make sure there aren't any suckers from its rootstock taking over the plant.

Why do my rose bush flowers seem to have sealed up in a ball?

This is a problem actually called 'balling' which occurs when water gets into the petals, causing the flower to seal up. It particularly affects old-fashioned varieties and will only clear up in drier weather. Remove any affected flowers.

What clematis would you recommend to grow up a tree?

There are so many to choose from! Some clematis flower throughout the year and even have attractive seedheads. *Clematis montana rubens* is great for growing up old fruit trees. Large-flowered hybrids such as 'Nelly Moser' make lovely companions to climbing roses, and *Clematis viticella* 'Polish Spirit' is a superb clematis to grow into a deciduous shrub such as lilac.

I have been told that my clematis has died of clematis wilt. What is this, and how do I treat it?

Little is known about wilt, but it is thought to be caused by a fungus entering a damaged part of the stem at soil level. Symptoms can appear overnight, with whole plants suddenly collapsing. All affected parts of the plant must be removed and burnt and the remaining plant should be sprayed with a systemic fungicide such as Benlate. If a plant persistently wilts it is best removed and a new clematis planted in a different part of the garden, as wilt can be local to a particular spot. Try to buy the strongest-looking plants, which seem to be more resistant, or choose species clematis such as *alpina*, *montana* and *macropetala*, which aren't susceptible to wilt.

HERBACEOUS BORDERS

In the height of summer there's nothing quite like a herbaceous border overflowing with colourful plants. Such a beautiful sight often tempts people to create their own borders, not realizing that this can be a very labour-intensive form of gardening. The gardens at Great Dixter in East Sussex are renowned for their colourful herbaceous borders, which are the particular joy of owner Christopher Lloyd. Graham Rice asked Christopher for his advice on beautiful borders.

GRAHAM RICE:

'Your borders always seem to change at Dixter. Some people would think that it is too much like hard work!'

CHRISTOPHER LLOYD:

'There is a lot of work involved in good gardening, but it's rewarding and I enjoy it.'

'What do you have in mind when you plant your borders? Are there any principles that you follow?'

'The idea is to grow plants of any kind, whether they're shrubs, herbaceous plants, annuals, bulbs, tender perennials – anything that goes well together. The aim is to achieve a good variety in contrast and colour. A range of hardy perennials will give you masses of colour, while shrubs in the border will give you firmness of texture. Height is also important and can be achieved by growing plants such as clematis up a pole.'

'What about colour combinations such as those harmonious pastel shades that people are always going on about?'

'Well, they're all right, but you can have too much of them – they're very fashionable at the moment. I'm keen on bolder, more striking colour contrasts myself. A plant like the purple smoke bush (Cotinus coggygria 'Royal Purple') makes such an excellent backdrop to other plants in the border, especially if you put it with mauve buddleia and red hot poker (Kniphofia).

'Another thing that I think is rather nice is to have some taller plants at the front of the border. Books always tell you to plant tall things at the back and short

at the front, but I think it all looks rather stodgy. I like to use plants such as Verbena bonariensis, which can grow to around 5 ft [1.5 m] and produces tufts of tiny purplish-blue flowers on tall, wiry stems in late summer. It makes a nice tall feature, and being quite a see-through plant it doesn't block the view.

'If you have a sheltered, sunny corner of the garden, why not create a tropical border? Plant the luxuriant-looking cannas, with their green or purple leaves and crimson flowers; castor oil plant (Ricinus communis 'Impala'), which produces deeply lobed bronze leaves; the giant reed grass (Arundo donax), with its broad, strap-like blue-green leaves up to 6 ft [1.8 m]; flowering tobacco (Nicotiana sylvestris), with its great big paddle leaves and white flowers; and angels' trumpets (Datura) for its strongly scented, trumpet-shaped, hanging flowers. Even bananas can thrive in a sheltered position, like the Japanese species (Musa basjoo), which also doesn't grow too tall. All these plants are more tender than your usual garden species, but the extra pampering they require is well worth the effort.'

Late-flowering borders

The arrival of spring is marked by an enthusiastic stampede to garden centres, where we happily fill up our trolleys with anything in flower. Although these plants look stunningly colourful for a few weeks there's a danger of creating a one-season garden, forgetting the golden rule that a well-planned garden has colour and interest all year round.

The easy way round this problem is to make regular visits to the garden centre throughout the year, so you can pick out colourful planting for every season. This could get expensive, so spend some time looking at gardening books first, and try to choose plants for a succession of flowers. When visiting other people's gardens throughout the year look for attractive plants in flower, and jot them down in a notebook or take a photograph of them. This will provide invaluable information for you later when you come to select plants for your own border.

Overleaf is a selection of some of the herbaceous plants that I admired for their late summer colour when I visited the beautiful grounds at Michelham Priory.

A pretty herbaceous border carefully planted in a pastel colour theme.

A DOWN-TO-EARTH GUIDE TO ENJOYABLE GARDENING

PLANT LISTS

Best late-flowering herbaceous plants

Coreopsis (tickseed): Masses of daisy-like flowers in colours ranging from yellow to pink.

Crocosmia (montbretia): Spikes of small, funnel-shaped, orange-red flowers and dramatic sword-like foliage. Particularly good is the variety 'Lucifer'.

Penstemon (beard tongue): Spikes of nodding, tubular flowers in various shades from white to purple-blue. Slightly tender, so it is worth taking cuttings.

Rudbeckia fulgida (black-eyed Susan): One of the finest plants for the autumn border and one of my favourites – in particular 'Goldsturm', with its daisy-like golden flowerheads with conical black centres.

Best border perennials

Achillea 'Moonshine': Large flat heads of sunny yellow flowers throughout summer.

Aster × *frikartii* 'Mönch': Lavender-blue daisy-like flowers in late summer and autumn.

Euphorbia characias wulfenii: A stately plant with huge clusters of yellow-green flowers lasting from spring to autumn.

Euphorbia polychroma: Low-growing, with long-lasting bright acid-yellow flowers in spring.

Geranium 'Wargrave Pink': Covered in bright salmon-pink flowers all summer.

Geranium wallichianum 'Buxton's Variety': Exceptional flowers, blue with a white centre, from mid-summer to autumn.

The beautiful leaves of *Hosta* 'Frances Williams'

Hosta 'Frances Williams': Huge sculpted leaves, blue-green with yellow edges. Avoid sun.

Kniphofia (red hot poker): Most common in shades of red, but an unusual pretty lemon-white variety is 'Little Maid'.

Paeonia 'Bowl of Beauty': Large open-cupped pink flowers, the centre crammed with blush-white pseudo-petals.

Sedum spectabile 'Autumn Joy': The best ice-plant, with large pink flowerheads fading to bronze in winter.

Geranium 'Wargrave Pink' is a perfect choice for the front of a border.

Golden rules for herbaceous borders

Some perennials (iris, for example) run out of steam after a few years – they grow into clumps and become overcrowded. To rejuvenate them, lift a whole group of plants with a fork, then divide the clump into small plants. Throw away the centre of the old clump and replant only new plants taken from around the edges. These younger plants will be strong and vigorous and will flower well.

As soon as the plants start into growth in the spring, support taller-growing varieties. Use metal supports (available from garden centres) or bamboo canes. Alternatively, and more cheaply, use pliable prunings from silver birch or hazel, stick them into the ground around the plant, and then bend the tops over to make a cage. If this is done early in the season the plant will grow up through the support and hide it completely.

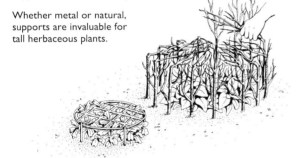

Whether metal or natural, supports are invaluable for tall herbaceous plants.

For a novel way of achieving height, grow a clematis or climbing rose up a pole in the middle of a border.

Herbaceous borders are greedy. Regular feeding and mulching will help to keep plants healthy and strong.

If you're trying to create a particular colour scheme, buy plants when they are in full flower so that you can be sure of getting exactly the colour you want.

Herbaceous questions and answers

What should I do with my lupins after they've flowered?

If you want to collect the seed for propagation, leave the faded flowers to form seedheads. Otherwise, remove each flowerhead as soon as it has finished to encourage more blooms. Once the plant has finished flowering, be brutal and cut the whole thing down to ground level. Within a few weeks it will sprout new shoots and you may even get a second crop of flowers. This also applies to other herbaceous plants such as delphiniums and hardy geraniums.

I would like to create a border to plant some shrubs and herbaceous perennials in, but I'm not sure how big it should be.

It obviously depends on how big your garden is, but even in a small garden the same rule applies: the bigger the better. Try to make your border as wide as possible, the minimum being 3 ft/90 cm – if it is too narrow your plants will look as though they are perched on a shelf. If your garden can take it, the ideal is 5 ft/1.5 m or more. This sounds like a large space to fill but it will give you far more flexibility with your planting, allowing you to grow taller shrubs at the back and more choice, scented flowers at the front.

How do I go about planting a herbaceous border?

Once you have selected your plants, place them on the prepared border in their pots to see where they would look best, and to get the spacings right. It is far easier to move a plant at this stage than it is once they are planted. Any plants that look particularly dry should be soaked, pot and all, in a bucket of water for an hour before planting. As a rule, herbaceous plants are planted in groups (preferably of odd numbers) to give a mass effect. Water in well, and your border will soon look established. If you decide later on that a plant is in the wrong place you can move it at virtually any time, even if it's in full flower. Water it well before lifting, dig it up with as much root as possible, and then give it another good drink when you've planted it in its new home.

My ground-cover geraniums begin to look a bit tatty after they've flowered in June. How can I prevent this?

Quite simply, cut them back to the ground after they've flowered. You'll be rewarded with a mass of fresh green leaves and usually another flush of flowers.

BEDDING PLANTS

It never ceases to amaze me how much sheer flower power bedding plants provide. They'll go on blooming quite happily for months on end just so long as you feed and water them regularly and, for most varieties, keep up a regular deadheading routine.

Some gardeners are a bit sniffy about bedding plants but I love them, and so does leading guru Christopher Lloyd, who advises experimentation, trying new combinations and new plants each year. While Christopher grows his from seed, most people rely on garden centres and Graham Rice visited Pat Wakely in West Sussex to give her some advice on what to buy. Pat had several corners of her garden that needed filling in and brightening up for the summer, so Graham showed her how to go about selecting the right plants for these spots.

GRAHAM RICE:

'There was a time when you went to a garden centre or nursery and found all the bedding plants sold in mixed colours — mixed antirrhinums, mixed marigolds, mixed everything. It was daft, really, because if you're decorating the living room you don't go and buy mixed rolls of wallpaper, do you?'

PAT WAKELY:

'No, that's true.'

'In recent years plants have become available in single colours. This means that you can now choose exactly which colour you want to go in a particular part of the garden, or to harmonize with an existing colour scheme. It also gives you the option to make up your own colour combinations. For example, if you fancied something in soft pastel colours, then you might look at the varied range of shades found in busy Lizzies (Impatiens). A tray of white busy Lizzies, a tray of pale pink and a tray of pale mauve would give you a lovely, subtle combination.

'Of course, for something a bit more garish, you could go for a more violent mix like deep reds, purples and yellows. But the point is that the choice is yours. You can do exactly as you like to suit your own tastes.'

'So what about my garden? Any recommendations for that bare bit of soil under my climbing rose?'

'How about a lovely scented-leaved geranium (Pelargonium quercifolium)? The flowers are not as flamboyant as some of the other geraniums, but they are quite pretty. The best thing is the smell of the leaves when crushed — they have a sort of minty, citrus aroma.'

'Mmmm, they smell lovely! I would never have thought of using a scented geranium.'

'Well, I think that a group of these geraniums would do really well in that hot, sunny spot at the base of your climbing rose. But what about your bush roses?'

'Well, I know that the bushes are getting on a bit and are now quite leggy and bare, but they still give me lots of flowers every year. What I'd like are a few suggestions as to what I can grow at the base of these plants to cover up their bare lower stems.'

'Again, the border they're growing in is in a sunny spot. The soil looks quite dry, so whatever you plant will be competing for water with the roses. We need to choose something that likes a sunny, dry spot and that will also hide those bare stems. I think the perfect choice would be Helichrysum petiolare. With its small grey downy leaves, it makes a tumbling mass of growth that will quite happily sprawl up your roses. The great thing about silver foliage plants is that they harmonize so well with virtually any flower colour. They'll be perfect with your roses.'

'Sounds great! How many of them would I need?'

'It depends on the size of your border, but as a general rule helichrysum needs to be planted about 9 inches [23 cm] apart. From this you will be able to work out how many you'll need. I'd also suggest Pelargonium 'Chocolate Peppermint', whose broad leaves would contrast well with the narrow leaves of the neighbouring flag iris and Hemerocallis (day lily), and Argyranthemum frutescens (marguerite), whose delicate foliage and flowers would contrast with the broad leaves of an autumn-flowering sedum.'

Right: The oak-leaved geranium (*Pelargonium quercifolium*) has the bonus of strongly scented leaves as well as attractive flowers.

THE ORNAMENTAL GARDEN

GRASS
ROOTS

Bedding plant questions and answers

Can you tell me what is wrong with my verbena plant, which seems to be flowering poorly and is covered in grey stuff?

Your plant is suffering from a disease called grey mould that is very common among many summer bedding plants. It usually appears when the weather is very wet and humid during the growing season. The spores of this mould spread on the wind; they can affect a plant as soon as they touch it, and can get in through a damaged leaf or stem. The mould will also quickly appear on decaying flowers, so the best cure is to practise good garden hygiene. Remove dead flowers, leaves and weeds (they can also be attacked) and burn them, along with any mouldy flowers as they appear. As a preventative measure, spray your plants as soon as they come into flower with a systemic fungicide. Otherwise, pray for drier weather!

Can you tell me how to grow hardy annuals?

Hardy annuals are simply sown directly into the border where they are to flower. In early spring, dig over the soil and add a little fertilizer. Draw blocks, or 'drifts', with lines of sand or a stick, and sow your seeds in straight lines within these areas. This means that when they germinate you will easily be able to spot which are annuals and which are weeds. Make the rows 6–8 inches/15–20 cm apart and thin the plants to similar distances when they germinate.

This dazzling display of hybrid verbenas couldn't fail to brighten up a dull border.

I'd like to cheer up a rather shady corner of my garden near the house. The soil is good, so are there any colourful bedding plants you could recommend?

Many of the bedding plants we naturally associate with a sunny spot will also tolerate all but the deepest shade. For height, you might like to use fuchsias – bright red, pink or white varieties would stand out well. Tobacco plants (*Nicotiana*) also like shade, and many are beautifully scented. And as an edging, you can't beat the cheerful little flowers of busy Lizzies (*Impatiens*).

I always plant my winter-flowering pansies in the same spot and they've always flourished until last year, when they didn't do well at all. What could be the reason?

The most likely cause is pansy sickness, a harmful fungus which builds up in soil where pansies or violets have been grown for some years. The most obvious symptoms are discoloration and wilting of the leaves and flowers. Unfortunately the soil remains infected for several years, so you will have to find a new spot for your pansies.

Golden rules for bedding plants

Don't be tempted into buying your plants too early. Garden centres have half-hardy plants for sale long before it is warm enough to plant them out. Unless you have a cool greenhouse to put them in for protection, wait until the threat of frost has passed in your particular area.

When planting in a border, take time to prepare the ground well. Dig in lots of organic matter and rake over the bed to create a fine soil.

To keep your display full of flowers throughout the summer, regularly pick off the dead blooms. This channels the plant's energies into producing even more flowers.

Feed bedding plants regularly with a high-potash fertilizer like liquid tomato food for even better results.

Buying enough plants for your garden can be expensive, so have a go at growing some from seed. Raise plants in pots on sunny windowsills for planting out or, if you're short of space, just grow hardy annuals, which can be sown directly into the spot where you want them to flower.

PLANT LIST

Best bedding plants

Bedding geranium 'Multibloom' series: Compact, uniform plants, which can produce up to 10 flowerheads at a time.

Begonia 'Non-Stop' series: Non-stop dazzling colour, huge blooms. The tubers can be lifted and stored.

Impatiens 'Accent' series: Vigorous, large-flowered busy Lizzies. Lovely colours and outstanding performance. Useful for shady spots.

Lobelia 'Cambridge Blue': Long-flowering, and a wonderful sky blue. Plant in large groups for maximum impact.

Mimulus 'Malibu' (monkey flower): Fast-growing, prolific flowers. Best in a shady spot – they hate drying out.

'Universal' pansies: Universal favourites for winter bedding, these come in a wide colour range. They sulk in severe weather but soon recover.

Busy Lizzies are reliable and colourful bedding plants.

CHAPTER THREE

THE
EDIBLE GARDEN

One of the highlights of my garden visits was a trip I made to Kent to meet a remarkable pair of brothers, the Fosbraey twins. To say that they like potatoes is something of an understatement – they're crazy about them, so much so that they have devoted the whole of their two allotments to their quest to find the perfect potato.

The twins had decided to plant a staggering 25 different varieties and, on top of that mammoth task, to experiment with alternative growing methods. It cheered me no end to learn that these practical, down-to-earth gardeners had discovered that the simplest method, the no-dig technique, had worked the best. Most people are wary about growing vegetables because they are considered to be difficult and time-consuming, but the Fosbraeys have proved otherwise (and they have also discovered the perfect potato, as you'll see on page 53).

To be fair, some vegetables such as cauliflowers are hard work and should only be grown by committed gardeners, but others, like onions, garlic and leaf beet, will quite happily fend for themselves. The key to successful vegetable-growing is being selective about what you grow, particularly if you are short of space and pushed for time.

Left: Vegetable gardens can be colourful and productive, as Michelham Priory shows.

I haven't as much space as I would like, so I concentrate on growing vegetables like peas, carrots and sweetcorn which taste mouthwatering when cooked straight from the garden. Other good varieties, such as the tangy tomato 'Gardener's Delight', I grow in pots. However, if you're lucky enough to have more room available, it may surprise you to know that a recent trial has shown that a 60–120 sq yd/50–100 sq m vegetable plot can be looked after in just two hours a week. Admittedly, those gardeners used every trick in the book to help them – like seep hoses for watering, adding plenty of organic compost in winter and, most importantly, keeping the weeds down by mulching – but they have proved it is possible to grow a wonderful selection of vegetables without slogging for hours.

When it comes to enthusiastic vegetable growing, you can't beat Joy Larkcom. Inspired by her extensive travels around the world, she has pioneered the introduction of new varieties and growing techniques. Joy has a passion for salad crops, and I was intrigued to discover that she grows many as 'cut and come again'. Tasty young plants of fast-growing varieties can be snipped to provide a delicious and colourful salad and then left to regrow. Joy reckons that up to three pickings can be obtained over a three-month period, and explains how simple it all is on pages 53–4.

Apparently only one in three people grow fruit in their garden. They are put off, I suspect, by the feeling that it's something of a mystical art – a feeling encouraged by gardening magazines which carry lengthy articles on pruning techniques and give daunting lists of pests and diseases which are enough to frighten anyone off. Don't be discouraged – some fruits, like blackberries, are so easy they almost grow themselves. And even apples are getting simpler – there are Ballerina trees which don't require pruning, a self-fertile 'Cox's Orange Pippin', and varieties so small you can step over them. And if space is really limited, what about growing some pots of strawberries on the windowsill in spring? For further ideas and inspiration on fruit growing, turn to pages 56–60.

At his home in Berkshire, Sir Terence Conran has created a stunningly pretty kitchen garden with rows of vegetables jostling for space with swathes of flowers. Just outside this walled garden is a neat and rather large herb bed. When I expressed surprise that he needed to grow so many, Sir Terence told me that they were picked daily and sent to London for the chefs to use ultra-fresh in his restaurants.

Slightly down the culinary scale, I've rescued many a disastrous meal by quickly adding some fresh herbs. I'm pleased to say that my cooking has improved tremendously since I met up with Ned Trier, who runs day courses on inspirational herb cookery. On page 63 Ned passes on one of his favourite recipes to celebrity gardener Alan Titchmarsh.

Apart from their culinary uses, herbs are particularly attractive foliage plants to grow in their own right. Most of them do best in sun on a light, well-drained soil, although some varieties like chives and borage can cope with heavier soils and partial shade. If your soil is a bit lumpy, just grow them in pots instead. Arrange the smaller herbs, like thyme and marjoram, around larger plants such as rosemary or bay, and cluster the pots together to make a decorative mini-garden.

The other good thing about herbs is that it doesn't cost much to start off a collection. Varieties like parsley and basil are easily raised from seed, while perennials such as thyme can be bought in small pots for growing on – and with any luck you'll have change from a £5 note. If you need any further persuasion, herbs are miraculously pest- and disease-free – the ideal plants for the laid-back gardener.

I hope that having read this you're now determined to have a go at growing yourself some edibles. They'll add a whole new dimension to your garden (just think of the apple blossom droning with bees), and you'll have a much better choice of varieties which taste fresher and better than any you can buy in the shops. Go on, spoil yourself.

VEGETABLES

In 1992 two of Kent's gardening characters, the Fosbraey twins, launched a trial to discover the ultimate in potatoes. Most of us would be content to leave it at that, even assuming we had room to try 25 varieties, but not the Fosbraeys — they decided to experiment with different growing techniques as well.

They grew potatoes in a variety of ways: in a potato barrel, where tubers are continually covered with manure as they grow; in trenches filled with manure with a 3-inch/7.5-cm plastic pipe sticking out of the ground next to each tuber, making it easy to get liquid feed straight to the potato; and in a 'no-dig' bed. All included their magic ingredient — turkey manure, three times richer in nitrogen, phosphorus and potassium (needed for healthy shoot, fruit and root development) than other farmyard manures. Much to everyone's delight, the twins discovered that they obtained the biggest crops from the no-dig beds.

JOHN FOSBRAEY:

'In late summer cover a large area of the garden with a 6-inch [15-cm] layer of rotted manure. When this has been well soaked by the rain, cover it all with black polythene and only remove it when the tubers are to be planted. Covering the ground with polythene smothers and kills any weeds, and encourages worms to take the manure into the soil; it also helps to warm up the soil and gives the potatoes a better start. Then simply push the tubers gently into the manure, about 12 inches [30 cm] apart, and cover them with a layer of well-rotted manure. This quick and simple method produces a great yield and is perfect if you have heavy clay soil because there is no digging involved.'

In case you're wondering which was the best of all the varieties they grew, the Fosbraeys decided that 'Desirée' was a good all-rounder, but for boiled potatoes they plumped for 'Pink Fir Apple'. This variety is rarely stocked by garden centres but is available from specialists. It's well worth keeping your eyes peeled for it.

Joy Larkcom is an enthusiastic pioneer of new ideas for vegetable-growing, testing out at her own market garden in Suffolk techniques she has discovered during

The unusually shaped 'Pink Fir Apple'.

her travels. She loves growing oriental varieties, which she plants alongside traditional vegetables and flowers. She explained to allotment holder Alex Rees that, with a bit of imagination and some packets of seeds, your salads need never be boring again.

JOY LARKCOM:

'I love the idea of having a salad that's a mixture of colours and textures as well as full of taste. You can even add a few flowers.'

ALEX REES:

'I had no idea you could eat flowers!'

'Lots of flowers are edible and they really add a splash of colour. They are all easy to grow, like the ordinary double daisy (Bellis perennis) with its pink petals, the orange pot marigold (Calendula), and the brightly coloured petals of nasturtiums and pansies — just sprinkle on a few petals to brighten up your salad. I'm also keen on salad seedlings. Once your crop has germinated, simply cut them off when they reach 1 inch [2.5 cm] high and eat them straight away.'

'Will they grow again?'

'Oh, yes, and the crop will grow back even thicker. Mustard and cress are ideal for growing in this way and can be sown in the usual narrow drill. I prefer to sow in a

much wider drill, though, so that you get a mass of seedlings to cut. Prepare your soil by forking it over and incorporating some well-rotted manure. Rake it so that it is nice and fine and then you can begin to sow.

'You can use an onion hoe, which has a wide blade. I prefer to use my favourite hoe, which is Chinese and has a hoe on one side and a rake on the other. Make a drill about 4 inches [10 cm] wide and only 1 inch [2.5 cm] deep then make another one right next door to it, as close as you can. All you need to do is press the seeds in lightly and rake over just enough soil to cover them — it's very quick. Once they germinate you will get a carpet effect with the seedlings tumbling from one row to the next.'

'And how long before I can start harvesting them?'

'Depending on what you've grown, you will usually be able to start cutting in about three weeks.

'Another thing that's fun is Oriental Saladini, a mix of seeds of Chinese brassicas that I find perfectly suited to growing in the carpet method. They are a collection of leafy greens with names like 'Komatsuna' and 'Mibuna'.

An onion hoe can be used to make a wide drill.

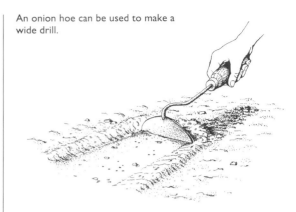

They are very hardy and very prolific and can be cut when they are little seedlings, about 2–3 inches [5–7.5 cm] high. If you leave them unthinned they can eventually grow into big plants up to 18 inches [45 cm] across — ideal for cooking and stir-frying. They are really productive and can go on supplying you with leaves for as long as four months. They will eventually go to seed, but even then they can still be of use as the flowers they produce can be eaten as they come into bud.'

The variegated nasturtium *Tropaeolum* 'Alaska Mixed' adds colour to the garden and the kitchen.

Vegetable questions and answers

I have just planted cabbages on my allotment. Is it true that planting marigolds between them will deter pests?

Tagetes is the most commonly used marigold – the strong smell of the flowers and foliage is said to deter many pests. When it is planted among tomato plants, the smell is reputed to keep away whitefly. Some people use the pot marigold (*Calendula*). This doesn't have such a potent smell, but it does attract the hoverfly whose larvae are great aphid eaters. Either way, marigolds are a must!

I have heard that deep-beds are a great way to grow vegetables in a small garden. What are they and how do they work?

Deep-beds are narrow strips of land no more than 4 ft/1.2 m wide with lots of manure, garden compost or spent mushroom compost dug in. This makes them very fertile, increases the depth of the soil for plants to root into and allows crops to be grown much closer together. The secret is not to tread on the beds as all the work can be done from the sides. As the soil is not compacted the drainage is improved, which means that the soil warms up quicker in spring and crops can be sown earlier.

Why has the garlic that I planted last spring failed to produce any bulbs?

The key to success with garlic is to plant your cloves in the autumn, as they need a period of cold in the early stages for bulbs to develop. Give them similar conditions to onions – good, well-drained soil in a sunny spot – and you should be harvesting fat, juicy bulbs the following autumn.

Is it true that if you remove the flowers from a potato plant you will improve the crop?

There is no evidence to say that this is true, so it is best to leave well alone. To ensure you have a good crop, water during dry spells because lack of moisture will check the plant's growth.

Can you give me some advice on storing vegetables to last through the winter?

Lift and store root vegetables such as parsnips before the ground freezes solid. Store them in wooden boxes (like those that fruit are sold in at markets) bedded on dry sand or compost. Put them in layers, making sure they are not touching. Cover with a final layer of sand and store the box in a frost-free shed.

Although time-consuming to prepare, a rope of onion or garlic is an ideal storage method, since there is less chance of disease spreading. Alternatively, hang them in nets – but this is far less attractive!

Onions can be woven together to form an onion rope. Again, store them somewhere frost-free. Make sure any vegetables you are going to store are not damaged in any way. Damaged ones will only rot, so use them immediately or throw them away.

Golden rules for vegetables

○ Aim to grow a succession of vegetables throughout the year. This usually involves a lot of clever planning and some good organization, but in simple terms can just mean sowing lettuce every couple of weeks in summer to give you a constant supply. Don't worry if you end up with hundreds of plants one week and none the next – even the most experienced gardeners don't always get it right!

○ Plant runner beans up a wigwam of garden canes and intermingle some sweet peas. Not only will they brighten up the vegetable patch, the sweet peas will attract bees which will then pollinate your runner beans.

Giving your vegetables some protection from the weather will allow them to reach full maturity at the end of the season and crop earlier in the spring. Use cloches made from glass, plastic or polythene. Placed over the soil a couple of weeks before sowing, the cloches will also help to warm up the soil, improving germination.

Picking your crop at the right time can mean the difference between a tasty meal and a tough, unpalatable vegetable. Many vegetables are tastier if they are picked young. Some varieties lose their freshness all too quickly when harvested, so cut them as you need them and eat them straight away.

PLANT LIST

Best vegetables

Carrot 'Amsterdam Forcing': Sweet finger carrots, maturing very early.

Courgette 'Gold Rush': Attractive golden fruits. High-yielding over a long period.

French bean 'The Prince': Long slim pods, superb flavour. Very prolific.

Lettuce 'Tom Thumb': A sweet, crisp and quick-maturing butterhead variety. Very compact.

Onion 'White Lisbon': A quick-growing spring onion type. Useful grown as winter salad crop.

Potato 'Pink Fir Apple': The supreme salad potato, with firm, waxy flesh and unbeatable flavour.

Radish 'French Breakfast': Cylindrical in shape, crisp and mild-flavoured. Good as a catch-crop between other vegetables.

Runner bean 'Scarlet Emperor': Heavy crops of long smooth beans. One of the best-flavoured runners.

The prolific, heavy-cropping and colourful courgette 'Gold Rush'.

Snap pea 'Sugar Bon': Fleshy 'eat-all' pods, crispy and sweet. Very compact variety.

Tomato 'Gardener's Delight': Hundreds of delicious red cherry tomatoes from one plant.

FRUIT

If you've been put off growing fruit because your garden is too small or because you've been told it's awfully complicated, I hope that the *Grass Roots* guide to fruit growing will help to change your mind. There's something magical about picking a sun-warmed pear off the tree or gathering bowlfuls of your own home-grown strawberries to enjoy for tea – and they'll taste so much better than anything you've ever bought in the shops.

Like many of the other plantings we've discussed, the key to success is careful planning when deciding which varieties to grow. I know it's tempting to rush into the garden centre and buy the first variety that's got a name you recognize, but it may well not be the best one for your garden.

The first consideration is how much space you have available. Apples, for instance, are grown in a number of different forms and the smallest of these you can actually step over. The extremely dwarf bushes are the next size up, growing to around 5 ft/1.5 m. These, like all other forms of apples, are grown on a special root-stock that controls the height of the mature tree. The M27 rootstock does best in good soil and you can pick up to 22 lb/10 kg of fruit a year.

Moving up the scale, there are 10 ft/3 m high bushes which grow on M9 rootstock. This is a good general choice for a smallish apple tree and they can yield up to 44 lb/20 kg of fruit.

For larger gardens, consider the M26 rootstock or the even bigger M106, which grows to 16½ ft/5 m but carries a bumper 110 lb/50 kg of fruit.

Having bravely decided that you have space to cram in an apple tree, you'll probably be horrified to be told at the garden centre that you need to plant two compatible varieties to cross-pollinate each other. The way round this is either to choose a 'family apple' – a tree onto which two or three varieties are grafted – or to team your tree up with a crab apple. These are highly decorative small trees, and 'John Downie' and 'Golden Hornet' are excellent pollinators.

Then it's down to which variety to grow. Just because you enjoy the taste of a particular shop-bought apple doesn't necessarily mean it's going to be the best one for your garden. 'Cox's Orange Pippin' is actually difficult to grow well – a variety called 'Sunset' is better and crops far more reliably. Likewise, a good alternative to the ubiquitous Bramley cooker is 'Bountiful', which has a sweeter flavour, a neater habit and is also mildew-resistant.

Plant your tree in good compost in a well-drained soil (they hate to be waterlogged), avoiding frost pockets if you can, and you'll be assured of good crops. Apples benefit from an annual prune and for trained forms, such as cordons, it's far simpler than you think, as Matthew Biggs explains on pages 125–8.

Pears are much less popular than apples and are trickier to grow well, especially in colder districts. As with apples, you will need two varieties for good pollination. They're usually supplied on Quince 'A' rootstock which grows to around 10 ft/3 m, and 'Concorde', 'Beth' and the delicious 'Conference' are generally considered the best.

Cordons are an easy way to grow a number of fruit varieties in a limited space.

Plums are far more easy-going and, what's more, they usually crop well without any pruning at all. The St Julien 'A' rootstock restricts their eventual height to 16½ ft/5 m with 55 lb/25 kg of fruit, while Pixy rootstock is smaller at 10 ft/3 m with 22 lb/10 kg of fruit. The variety 'Victoria' is self-fertile and still one of the best.

Luckily most of the cherries are also self-fertile, though even one tree takes up a good deal of space. They're ideal to grow against a wall, but you'll need to protect them from birds when they fruit.

I'm rather partial to peaches, but they do need a warm spot to grow well. The ideal position is against a sheltered wall, where they can be covered with a polythene lean-to for the six months from mid-winter in order to prevent the disfiguring disease peach leaf curl. The ends should be left open to allow for good ventilation and access by pollinating insects. All in all, it is a bit of a chore.

Soft fruit needs less room in the garden and my favourite is still the strawberry, which can be grown in pots or growing bags. One of the neatest ways of growing them in the ground is through polythene,

The mouth-watering red fruits of the 'Victoria' plum.

Raspberries are an easy and very rewarding fruit to grow.

which keeps the soil moist and smothers weeds. For a succession of fruit, plant more than one variety – about six plants of each will give a good crop. 'Honeoye' is the best early variety and 'Hapil' is a succulent high-yielding summer variety.

For many people the best soft fruit is the raspberry, but it does need some space. It's best to grow the plants in rows, trained on wires. Although they generally crop in the summer, a newer variety called 'Autumn Bliss' gives a good yield in late summer and is easier to look after than other varieties – you simply cut all the canes to ground level in spring. Eight plants should be sufficient for a family of four.

Blackberries are probably the simplest of the soft fruit to grow, and 'Loch Ness' is a particularly good choice. It is thornless, carries heavy crops of up to 22 lb/10 kg and is very compact, growing to just over half the height of other blackberry varieties, so requires little or no support.

Gooseberries are quite hard work, but 'Invicta' is a high-yielding variety that will make it worth your while. Currants are much easier, once you've mastered the pruning techniques, and well worth finding space for since they're less readily available in the shops. 'Red Lake' is a good redcurrant and 'Ben Sarek' a heavy-cropping, fairly compact blackcurrant.

To get the best from your fruit give it an annual spring feed, using fish blood and bone for all types except strawberries, which prefer potash. Mulch it to keep the weeds down, water it in very dry spells, and don't forget the pruning. It's nowhere near the hard work it sounds and once you've tasted the fruits of your success you won't regret a minute of it.

The prolific and disease-resistant apple 'Pixie'.

PLANT LISTS

Best fruit

As nominated by world-renowned apple expert Dr Joan Morgan.

Apple 'Pixie': Small striped fruit of excellent flavour. Heavy, reliable cropper, easy to grow and keeps until March.

Apple 'Sunset': Fine aromatic flavour. Related to 'Cox's Orange Pippin' but much hardier. Ready to eat late autumn.

Pear 'Conference': Very juicy and sweet. The most reliable of all pears, ripening mid-October.

Pear 'Doyenne du Comice': Succulent flesh, unsurpassed for flavour, but needs good soil and a sheltered site.

Plum 'Cambridge Gage': Green-fleshed and very juicy, with a rich, sweet taste. Good cropper.

Best soft fruit

As nominated by fruit expert Ken Muir.

Blackberry 'Loch Ness': Thornless, non-rambling, with large, tasty fruit produced on stout upright canes. Ideal for small gardens.

Blackcurrant 'Ben Sarek': Very compact bushes with extremely heavy crops of large, well-flavoured fruit.

Gooseberry 'Invicta': Vigorous and healthy, with large crops of smooth, pale green berries, excellent for cooking, freezing and jam.

Raspberry 'Glen Moy': Compact, thornless, with a fine flavour. Crops in June, with a second small crop on the young canes in autumn.

Strawberry 'Hapil': A reliable mid-summer variety, with good yields of large, conical, bright red fruit. Very good flavour.

Golden rules for fruit

Pick fruit only when it is ready. Don't pull it from the branch but lift it up to the horizontal; if it is ripe it should simply twist off.

Make sure that when you plant fruit trees the join between the rootstock and the variety (the bend in the bottom of the stem) is high enough above the ground and any mulch to stop the variety from taking root. As the rootstock controls the vigour of the tree, it is important not to let the variety take root or your tree could suddenly start growing out of control, and your carefully chosen dwarf variety could sprout into a giant!

If you fancy something a little exotic, grow a fig tree (*Ficus carica*). It will do well if given the shelter of a south- or west-facing wall, or even a cold greenhouse or conservatory. Small fruits will then develop and swell during the winter to ripen the following summer.

Strawberries are always a firm favourite and their flowers can be attractive too. Plant the variety 'Serenata' and you will have pretty pink flowers as well as plenty of fruit.

If you're picking fruit for storage, be careful to select good specimens. Pears are best stored individually. Up to 6$\frac{1}{2}$ lb (3 kg) of apples can be stored in a plastic bag (make some holes in it first).

Fruit questions and answers

I have been growing strawberries for a number of years and the crop has slowly deteriorated. Where am I going wrong?

Generally, once they have been cropped for three years, strawberries should be replaced. Anchor down some runners from the mother plants and when they have rooted cut them off and plant them in a new strawberry bed.

New strawberry plants are simply grown from runners.

Which variety of fruit tree would you recommend to grow from a pip?

Growing trees like apples and pears from pips is really a waste of time if you want a tree that fruits well – the only one that is worth growing is a peach. Germinate the stone in a pot and wait until the plant is established before planting it in a sheltered part of the garden against a south-facing wall, or in a well-ventilated cold greenhouse.

How can I tell if my plum tree is suffering from silver leaf disease?

Shiny silver foliage suggests that a tree may be suffering from this serious fungal disease. The easiest way to tell is to scrape the bark of an affected branch; if the stem is stained brown, then it is silver leaf. It only affects one part of the tree, whereas a similar-looking (but not so serious) condition called false silver leaf affects the whole plant. If it is silver leaf, prune out affected branches 6 inches/15 cm below the infection, mulch your tree in autumn with rotted horse manure and foliar feed in spring, and it should grow out of this condition. Only in very bad cases when bracket-like toadstools have appeared will the tree have to be destroyed. False silver leaf is usually a sign that the tree is undernourished, so a programme of regular feeding and mulching with horse manure should help the tree improve.

What type of apple tree would you recommend for a small garden?

Cordons are ideal if you have limited space and are decorative as well as being highly productive. They consist of a single stem which is trained at an angle to slow down the flow of sap and channel energy into fruiting. Fruit is produced on short spurs along the length of the stem where it can be easily picked. Grow them against a fence or wall, or freestanding on wires and posts.

HERBS

Despite their undoubted value, herbs are still sadly underrated by many gardeners. They are easy to grow and many varieties, for example the neat golden thyme, are among the prettiest of plants. And, of course, the culinary varieties can transform even the humblest dish into something mouthwateringly tasty.

Alan Titchmarsh took a walk around Hollington Herbs with owner Simon Hopkinson.

Sir Terence Conran's beautifully designed, ornamental kitchen garden.

ALAN TITCHMARSH:

'Is it true that the coloured forms of herbs like fennel and sage have just as much flavour as the plain green ones?'

SIMON HOPKINSON:

'You'll generally find that the flavours in either form are virtually the same. The useful thing with coloured herbs is that if you haven't got room for a serious herb garden you can dot your plants among a flower border, where they will look lovely while being edible as well. There are plants like the coloured sages (Salvia officinalis), for example the purple-splashed 'Purpureum' and 'Icterina', with variegated pale green and yellow leaves; the tall feathery foliage of purple fennel (Foeniculum vulgare 'Purpureum'); and the many mints (Mentha) with leaves splashed with cream and tinged with purple. With so many to choose from, you can't fail to find one that will fit into a border.'

Herb questions and answers

How can I stop mint from taking over my garden?

You have to be careful when planting mint as most varieties are very invasive, but it can be kept under control. Plant it in a bucket which has had its bottom removed. Plunge this into the soil but keep the bucket rim 2 inches/5 cm above the ground, otherwise the plant will spill out and soon take root in the surrounding soil. If planting in a border, dig a hole, line it with plastic which has had a few holes punched in it for drainage, fill the hole with soil and plant. The plastic will act as a barrier. If you want guaranteed control, plant your mint straight into a container like an old stone sink, large terracotta pot or oak barrel.

Can you tell me why my red bergamot (*Monarda didyma*) is not flourishing? It is growing in a container in a shady spot in the garden.

This tall perennial herb has broad, slightly toothed leaves and shaggy red flowers that appear from mid-summer. It does require an airy sunny position so move the pot into the sun, make sure you are feeding it well and it should improve. The leaves can be dried in mid-summer and infused to make a drink which closely resembles a scented China tea.

How can I make a standard bay tree, with a single bare trunk and a round ball-shaped head?

Take a young bay plant (*Laurus nobilis*) with a single leading stem. Cut off any side shoots and allow the

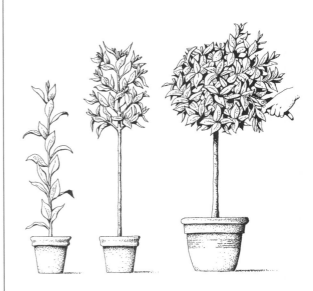

It takes time and patience to grow a bay tree as a standard. But considering the high prices they reach in garden centres, it's well worth all the effort.

leader to grow, continually removing side shoots as they develop. This single stem will become the trunk of your bay tree. Once it has reached the height you want your tree to be, pinch out the growing point. Decide how large you want the head or 'ball' of the tree to be, and then take off all the leaves from the trunk below, leaving you with a bare stem. Allow the side shoots of the head to grow but keep pinching them out to make the ball become bushy. Your standard bay tree will require a yearly trim to keep its shape.

Ned Trier, garden consultant and cook, illustrated how to use herbs in cooking by making one of his favourite recipes.

Rosemary and garlic bread

1½ lb/750 g strong plain flour
2 tsp salt
1 sachet easy-blend dried yeast
12 fl oz/350 ml warm water
3½ fl oz/90 ml olive oil
fresh rosemary sprigs
garlic cloves
sea salt

Put the flour and salt in a large bowl and sprinkle in the powdered yeast. Pour in three-quarters of the warm water and oil and mix to a dough. Add the rest of the liquid gradually to make a smooth dough that leaves the sides of the bowl clean. (You may not need all the liquid or you may need a spoonful more, as flours vary.)

Place the dough on a flat surface and knead until elastic. Cover the dough with a damp tea-towel or clingfilm and leave in a warm place to rise until double in size. Knead well and then shape the loaf, forming it into a round, slightly pizza-type shape just under 1 inch/2.5 cm thick. Place it on a well-greased baking sheet. With your fingers, make little dents on the surface of the bread and put fresh sprigs of rosemary and small cloves of garlic in alternate holes. Brush generously with olive oil and sprinkle with sea salt. Bake in a hot oven (230°C/450°F/Gas Mark 8) for 15–30 minutes. Eat while warm.

Common rosemary (*Rosmarinus officinalis*), one of the most popular and versatile of herbs.

An extremely stylish way of growing herbs, flowers and vegetables in a very small area. The grass seat is an optional extra!

Golden rules for herbs

Herbs are easy to grow indoors through the winter months. Sow annual herbs like basil and parsley in pots on windowsills towards the end of summer. Perennials, such as mint and chives, can be lifted and potted up in late summer. Allow the plants to become established in their pots before bringing them inside. Grow them on a sunny kitchen windowsill and you will have fresh herbs to pick all winter.

Although herbs are best used fresh, there are a number of ways in which you can store them for later use. Cut bunches of rosemary, thyme and sage in the morning, making sure that the foliage is dry. Tie them in bunches and hang them up to dry somewhere warm and dark. Once dry, the brittle leaves can simply be crumbled off into a clean airtight jar. Label the jar and store it in a cool, dark, dry cupboard. Herbs freeze well, so put bundles into bags in the freezer or chop the leaves up finely, put them into ice cube trays, add a little water and freeze.

If you want to bring the smell of your garden indoors, make your own pot-pourri. Use leaves from herbs like lavender, bay and myrtle and mix them with delphinium and rose petals, which can be dried on trays covered with newspaper. Mix your ingredients in a bowl and add orris root powder to fix the scent. Store in stoppered jars for six

Drying herbs ready for the winter.

weeks to allow the scents to mature. Pour the finished pot-pourri into an earthenware container with a well-fitting lid.

Try to plant your herbs as near to your kitchen door as possible. When you have to nip out for some herbs you won't want to have to trek halfway down the garden, particularly in the winter.

PLANT LIST

Best herbs – as nominated by Ned Trier.

Chervil: An underrated but delicious annual with lacy foliage and a sweet, delicate, aniseed taste.

Coriander: Wonderful, slightly oily flavour to the leaves, spicy seeds.

Dill: The classic ingredient for Swedish gravadlax, or as a flavouring for soups and pickles.

French parsley: Strong-flavoured flat parsley, infinitely superior to the curled variety.

French tarragon: Delicious leaves which combine to great effect with many chicken and egg situations.

Lemon thyme: A bushy little plant that goes well with many dishes. Bees love the flowers.

Marjoram: Try the variety 'Compactum', with pincushions of light green leaves.

Rosemary: An attractive shrub, covered in scented evergreen needles for use in breads and meat dishes.

Sorrel: Use in wonderful lemony soups or in sauce for salmon. Cut back to encourage tender young leaves.

Sweet basil: Well-loved both fresh and cooked. Grows best in large pots in a greenhouse or on a kitchen windowsill.

CHAPTER FOUR

CONTAINER GARDENING

A few years ago an enterprising village near Durham launched a flower show with a difference. Called 'The Alternative Flower Show', it featured some highly imaginative classes, including The Ugliest Houseplant, The Biggest Weed, and The Fruitcake with the Most Fruit at the Bottom. All the classes were popular, but the one that had the crowds flocking was The Most Unusual Plant Container. An amazing variety of receptacles had been conjured up, from washing-up bowls to shoes, and what's more the plants looked quite at home in them all.

Inspired by such innovative use of containers, I've started to be a bit more adventurous myself. I've tried old tyres and paint cans, but I've yet to plant up any of my old shoes (I'm still wearing them). As the villagers demonstrated so vividly, virtually anything can be used as long as it's waterproof. All you have to do is make drainage holes in the base, add a layer of gravel or broken pots and then fill in with a multi-purpose potting compost.

Once you've sorted out your pot, deciding what you're going to plant in it presents even more of a challenge. The good news is that virtually anything can be grown in a container. In fact, when I used to help with the displays at the Chelsea Flower Show, we took

Left: A simple, but bold, collection of pots creates a stylish effect.

A selection of potential plant containers, including my boots!

the same plants every year; all grown in pots for easy handling, they included anything from old-fashioned roses to massive trees. The annual *pièce de résistance*, incidentally, was a stunning wisteria, grown in a milk crate!

Don't restrict yourself to ornamental plants. How about a mini salad garden (colourful 'Lollo Rossa' lettuce with spring onions and radish) grown in a window box? You could even consider planting a golden courgette in a tub – the leaves and flowers are highly decorative, and you could pop in a few nasturtiums for extra colour.

Some varieties of fruit are also very suitable for containers, for example the upright maypoles of Ballerina apples, or apples grafted on to the very dwarfing M27 rootstock. Strawberries are ideal and, in fact, growing them in pots means they stand a fighting chance against slugs. And herbs positively revel in this treatment and often taste better – partly, no doubt, because of the extra heat generated by the pot.

If you're really stuck for inspiration, just buy a packet of easy-to-grow annual flower seeds. One of the simplest and most effective displays I've seen was a plastic pot overflowing with Californian poppies (*Eschscholzia*) grown from seed. It cost around £1 and looked stunning for months.

When autumn draws in, don't just abandon your containers – give them a fresh lease of life by planting bulbs. They're great value as well and, even better, almost foolproof to grow. On page 70 Adam Pasco has some excellent ideas for bulbs in containers.

One of the more wittily named classes at 'The Alternative Flower Show' was called Hanging's Too Good For It, and the entries included some of the most unusual hanging baskets I've ever seen. Growing good baskets is an undoubted skill, and one of the most important factors is your choice of plants. Some of the prettiest baskets are colour-themed. That's not as grand as it sounds – it basically means sticking to one or two colours such as hot crimson and orange, soft pink and white or fresh yellow and blue to create some wonderful effects. Kathleen Brown specializes in growing the most eye-catching hanging baskets and on page 74 she passes on her recipe for success.

Be a bit bold – don't just stick to well-tried formulas such as lobelia, geraniums and petunias. How about an edible basket crammed full of strawberries and herbs or the lovely tomato 'Tumbler'? And do have fun experimenting with new plants. Last year I was delighted with the semi-trailing petunia 'Surfinia' which I grew in a hanging basket by the door. Unfortunately it grew so huge that my wife, tired of fighting her way in and out, made me cut it back. So be warned, only plant this particular new variety where you've plenty of space.

Once you have planted your containers and baskets they must be nurtured. It's essential to water and feed them regularly and, to be honest, watering's a real chore, particularly in the case of baskets. I always add water-retention crystals when I pot the plants up and line the sides of terracotta pots with polythene to reduce evaporation. Incidentally, clustering the pots together not only looks good but also helps to reduce water loss. The position of the container also affects the frequency of watering. Hostas, for instance, will grow very happily in shade and need far less water. Other plants which prefer sun should, if possible, be placed where they'll receive only morning or late afternoon sun; in a fully exposed south-facing position they'll dry out in a flash.

There is, fortunately, a way of making feeding easier – just add some slow-release fertilizer when you plant, then sit back and forget about it. If only all gardening were so simple!

So in future I hope you'll be seeing your old mop bucket in a new light. Container gardening is a terrific opportunity to experiment on a small scale, so have fun, try different containers, new plants and unusual plant associations and be as outrageous as you like.

Right: A traditionally planted and extremely colourful hanging basket, which should look good all summer long.

BULBS

Spring bulbs are the eighth wonder of the world, or so it always seems when they emerge fresh and bright to put a full stop to the grim winter months. Most are tailor-made for containers, and will revel in the rich soil and good drainage. They're versatile, too, and can be used to add interest to permanent container plantings or to make glorious features in their own right when massed in pots.

Adam Pasco, editor of *Gardeners' World Magazine*, met bulb expert Christine Skelmersdale of Broadleigh Gardens bulb nursery to discuss the best ways of guaranteeing a brilliant spring display.

ADAM PASCO:

'Containers come in all shapes and sizes and are made from a variety of materials including concrete, wood, plastic and terracotta – make sure the latter are frostproof. Avoid using too small or too shallow a container, as in winter it could freeze solid. Check for good drainage holes, as bulbs hate wet soil. Plastic planters are cheap but they are often thin and have poor drainage, so the compost inside can freeze absolutely solid in winter.

'I would choose a terracotta pot with good drainage holes. So what's the next thing to consider?'

CHRISTINE SKELMERSDALE:

'Deciding what to plant! I like to keep it simple. With summer bedding, you have a wonderful display for four to five months. This doesn't happen with bulbs, as they produce one show of flowers and then it's all over in a fortnight. Plant only one variety of bulb in the pot and when it has finished flowering have another pot ready for the next fortnight.'

'How do you buy the best bulbs?'

'The best range will be from a specialist bulb-grower. They will send you bulbs of the ideal size at the right time for planting. Alternatively, go to a garden centre to choose from what's there. I like to buy bulbs in the same way I buy vegetables – if I can touch them I know exactly what I'm getting. Avoid buying bulbs in sealed bags where you can't see what's inside.

Make sure your pots have good drainage holes.

For top-quality bulbs, hand-pick them individually.

'Pick the bulbs up – they should look fat, firm and healthy and the base should be firm. This is the most important part, as it is where the roots come from.'

'Although bulbs are in the shops from the end of summer, do you think that is in fact the best time to buy them?'

'Yes, because you will have first choice and be able to pick the best and fattest bulbs. I'm not going to plant them yet as I don't want to disturb my summer pots, which are just coming into their glory – I'll keep them in the garage instead. I can store them a lot better than the garden centre can! Put your bulbs somewhere dry and airy – keep them in paper bags, never in polythene where they can sweat and go mouldy. Then, when you're ready to plant up in autumn, you've got the bulbs waiting for you.'

'Remember when you plant to put plenty of drainage materials such as broken pots, pebbles or gravel into the bottom of the container so that the compost drains well. I prefer to use one of the soil-based ones, such as John Innes, which has plenty of extra grit added to make it free-draining. Peat-based compost tends to get too wet or else to dry out completely.

'Put the compost in your pot, plant your bulbs and water them well. If the weather gets very cold, you can always move the pots to a sheltered part of the garden for protection.'

Bulb questions and answers

Why, after two years, are my daffodils not flowering?

Daffodils can become exhausted, so as soon as flowering is over give them a feed with a granular fertilizer. Alternatively, use a liquid feed every couple of weeks until the leaves show signs of yellowing and begin to die down. When this happens, about six to eight weeks after flowering, cut them off – don't do it any sooner or you'll affect the bulb's ability to flower. Don't tie the leaves in a knot, as it will only throttle the bulb and prevent it from being able to make the food it needs to flower next year.

Can you recommend a spring-flowering bulb suitable for growing in a small window box?

Try some of the smaller varieties of narcissi, such as 'Peeping Tom', growing 10–12 inches/25–30 cm, or *Narcissus bulbocodium*, which only grows to 6–8 inches/ 15–20 cm. Planted among winter-flowering heathers and pansies, they would be perfect to cheer up a dull winter's day.

Can you tell me how I can get hyacinths to flower for Christmas?

You must buy prepared bulbs which have had a special temperature treatment for earlier flowering. Plant them in bulb fibre in a pot with drainage holes, making sure the hyacinths have their tips just above the surface. Place them in a cool shady place until the shoots develop after 9 to 11 weeks.

When the shoots are 2 inches/5 cm high, move them into full light in a cool room. After three to four weeks, when the flower buds have formed, move the pot into a warmer position where you will be able to enjoy the fragrant blooms. (If you are too impatient and move it before the buds are formed you'll end up with a lot of leaves and stunted flowers.) The latest planting time in the UK if you want flowers for Christmas is 15 September.

Hyacinths are fun to grow in special glasses filled with water. Keep them cool, topping up with water as necessary. Move into a warm, light room when colour develops in the flower buds.

PLANT LIST

Best bulbs for containers

Anemone blanda: Low-growing, covered in white, pink or blue star-shaped flowers in March and April.

Crocus chrysanthus 'Blue Pearl': Soft lavender blue with white, around golden centres. Fragrant.

A clump of crocus flowers is a cheering sight in early spring.

Iris reticulata 'Joyce': Dwarf blue, beautifully marked. Ideal for window boxes, flowering January and February.

Muscari armeniacum (grape hyacinth): Can be rampant in the garden, but looks lovely in captivity in pots.

Narcissus 'Baby Moon': A delicate golden dwarf narcissus. Multi-headed, with lemony fragrance and reed-like leaves.

Narcissus 'Mount Hood': A tall milky-white daffodil, very striking. Avoid exposed positions.

Narcissus 'Tête-à-Tête': A short variety with scented golden blooms, two or three to a stem.

Tulipa 'Angélique': A tall double tulip coloured a lovely mix of candy-pink and white, resembling a peony.

Tulipa 'Black Parrot': A dramatic explosion of huge feathered crimson-purple flowers on tall stems.

Tulipa 'Shakespeare': A short variety, excellent for window boxes. Star-shaped red and salmon flowers with a yellow centre.

The strikingly different 'Black Parrot' tulip.

Golden rules for bulbs

When buying, choose healthy, large, firm bulbs. If they are not to be planted straight away, store them in paper bags (not plastic) in a dry, airy place.

Treat your bulbs as annuals. Once they have finished flowering and the leaves have died down, lift the bulbs and store them for planting next autumn. Your container can then be used for planting up with summer bedding.

If you have a neglected corner of your lawn, brighten it up with a spring carpet of naturalized bulbs such as crocus. Scatter a handful of bulbs across the lawn and plant them where they fall. Alternatively, cut the turf in an 'H' pattern, roll it back and fork the soil over. Add some bonemeal, scatter in the bulbs and then roll back the turf.

CONTAINERS

Container gardening gives you enormous scope for experiment. So think laterally — forget all the rules about what constitutes a suitable container plant (the answer is, just about anything), and remember that a container is simply a waterproof receptacle with drainage holes. A colander, for example, would fit the bill, except that it might be slightly too free-draining and watering could become a nightmare!.

Kathleen Brown, author and expert on container gardening, is bursting with fresh ideas, as I discovered when I met her to discuss some of her recipes for seasonal planting.

Themed plantings can make an effective and unusual display.

A DOWN-TO-EARTH GUIDE TO ENJOYABLE GARDENING

KATHLEEN BROWN:

'How about a spring hanging basket of herbs and flowers? Trap rampant growers like mint in a basket and they will be no trouble at all. Pick variegated ones, like applemint (Mentha suaveolens 'Variegata'), and plant them with violas and bellis daisies.

'I like to use unusual containers as well – old wicker baskets, for example. Most people would use them for shopping, but I think they look great when they're planted!'

RICHARD JACKSON:

'That's a wonderful idea, but how long would such a basket last outdoors in all weathers?'

'Well, I protect them with a coat of yacht varnish. Brush the whole basket inside and out with three coats of varnish, allowing each coat to dry completely before adding the next. It's important not to rush this job so that it's done properly. If a yacht can stay out all summer in the water, then a wicker basket should be all right for a few seasons.'

'How do you plant one up?'

'In the same way you would any other container, but

Preserving a wicker basket with yacht varnish.

remembering to line the basket with plastic which has had a few holes made in it for drainage.'

'What about some planting ideas for summer?'

'I like to think in recipe terms when I plant, making a list of ingredients to make it easier to do. For a summer container I might choose an upright red geranium for the centre, three scarlet trailing geraniums to go around the edge, and then fill in the gaps with parsley plants, with their lovely fresh green frilly foliage. Once planted, such a combination will be easy to look after and should be relatively pest-free.'

A well-planted window box can be a breathtaking sight.

PLANT LIST

Best plants for hanging baskets and window boxes

Begonia semperflorens: Cheery little flowers, constantly produced, in a lovely colour range.

Bidens aurea: Starry gold flowers freely produced against delightful ferny foliage.

Brachyscome: Filmy foliage studded with a succession of tiny daisy flowers in white, pink or blue.

Helichrysum petiolare: An invaluable grey-leaved trailer. 'Aurea' is a greeny gold form.

Lobelia 'Cambridge Blue': The best colour form.

A potentially dull area can be transformed by a colourful window box.

Lotus berthelotii: Silver filigree trailing foliage scattered with red pea-like flowers.

Pelargonium: Any of these tender geraniums will do well in hanging baskets and window boxes.

Petunia 'Surfinia': A wide-growing variety, producing up to ten times more flowers than others.

Tropaeolum majus 'Alaska' (nasturtium): Neat dwarf variety, the leaves attractively marbled with white.

Pansy: Wonderful choice of colours, very free-flowering if regularly dead-headed.

PLANT LIST

Best plants for pots and tubs

Acer palmatum: Any of the slow-growing Japanese acers make lovely specimen plants for partial shade.

Agapanthus: Rounded heads of blue flowers on tall arching stems, with long strap-shaped leaves.

Argyranthemum frutescens (marguerite): White daisy flowers on rounded bushes all summer.

Begonia, tuberous hybrids: A non-stop display of large double flowers in a wide colour range.

Fuchsia: Any will romp away in pots. 'Annabel' (pink) and 'Thalia' (red) are especially good. Keep well watered.

Hosta: Large-leaved varieties look splendid in pots, and are safe from slugs.

Lilium: All lilies look very striking in pots. Set scented varieties near doors.

Osteospermum (star of the veldt): Shimmering, large daisy flowers in pastel shades. Loves a sunny spot.

Phormium tenax (New Zealand flax): Makes a dramatic, spiky focal point. Give winter protection in colder areas.

Rosa: Any of the miniature roses will do well in pots, as well the smaller ground-cover varieties.

The versatile and beautiful marguerite (*Argyranthemum frutescens*).

Golden rules for containers

Make sure that whatever container you choose will stand up to cold winter weather – there's nothing more annoying than coming into the garden on a winter's morning to find a favourite pot in pieces on the terrace, and it won't do the plant any good either. Most terracotta pots are guaranteed frost-proof now, but ask before you buy.

When plants become too large to repot, remove the top few inches of soil in spring and replace it with fresh. Firm the compost in with your fingers and tap the sides of the pot so that any air pockets are filled. Give the pot a thorough watering.

Tall plants in containers are liable to topple over in strong winds. If plants are to go in an exposed spot, use heavy soil-based composts and large terracotta or stone pots to keep them stable. Alternatively, position them in a more sheltered site.

Keep costs down by recycling the polystyrene trays that plants are sold in at garden centres. They make excellent drainage material if broken up and put into the bottom of a pot. Growing bags are one of the cheapest sources of compost, although the more expensive multi-purpose composts usually produce better results.

Use a genuine cooper's barrel that has been cut in half to make an attractive small pond. The wood expands when the pond is full and becomes watertight. (If you're using a half tub from a garden centre it will need coating with bitumen to seal the joints.) Place in a sunny spot, fill with water and add a couple of marginal plants, a dwarf water lily and even a goldfish or two.

A mini-pond is easily created in a wooden half-barrel.

Container questions and answers

Why does my pot-grown hydrangea have yellow leaves?

Your plant may be lacking in nutrients; plants in pots need regular attention, especially in hot weather. Any fertilizer in the soil is soon used up, so feed your plants on a regular basis with a liquid fertilizer like sea-weed, and check if they need watering on a daily basis during the growing season. If necessary repot the whole plant in the spring.

How do I look after a sink garden that I have recently planted with alpines?

Alpine plants thrive in sink gardens but need free-draining soil, so put plenty of broken pots or gravel in the bottom of the container before planting and use a gritty soil-based compost. Water during the summer but only feed sparingly during the growing season – overfeeding will cause the plants to outgrow the sink, which will then have to be replanted. Alpines need an open sunny spot, so make sure your sink is in the right place before you plant it – once planted it may prove too heavy to lift.

I planted up my window box with good garden soil, but the plants have grown very poorly. What am I doing wrong?

Using garden soil in containers is a mistake many people make. Unless it is an extremely good soil and is mixed with compost and fertilizers, it is best avoided. You will have far better results from a bought compost, which will have the correct level of feed in it.

CHAPTER FIVE

HOUSEPLANTS AND CONSERVATORIES

On one occasion last year a lady came up to ask the secret of looking after houseplants. Normally I would have responded with a very traditional, straightforward answer but for the fact that the previous day I had been visiting scriptwriter Carla Lane, who shares her house and garden with the animals she has rescued. With the memory of Carla's happy menagerie still very fresh in my mind, I replied, 'Treat your houseplants like pets.'

As she looked at me in astonishment, I hurriedly explained my theory: give your houseplants warm and comfortable living quarters, remember to feed and water them regularly, groom them occasionally and by all means talk to them. Do all this and your plants will look sleek, contented and flourishing. The secret, of course, is that you're paying them lots of attention, so not only will you appreciate them more, you'll also be more responsive to their needs and spot any problems in the very early stages.

The lady had fled by this point, but I still think the analogy holds. Just as different pets have varying requirements so do houseplants, and it makes sense to discover what living conditions will suit them best. Plants such as ferns love moisture in the air, so it

Left: A conservatory provides an ideal environment for plants and people.

would be cruel (and disastrous) to keep them in a warm centrally heated sitting room. A humid bathroom would be far more sensible. Likewise, bedrooms are usually the best bet for flowering plants because they're generally cooler and lighter – ideal conditions for longer-lasting flowers.

Fortunately, most houseplants now come with a care card that gives information on light and temperature requirements, though they can be infuriatingly vague on watering. What on earth does 'water moderately' mean? It's enough to send anyone into a panic.

Of all the frustrating mysteries in the gardening world, houseplant watering is surely the one that worries new gardeners the most. The *Grass Roots* rule is 'If in doubt, don't'. More houseplants are killed through kindness (i.e. overwatering) than through neglect. You can buy gadgets to help you decide when to water, but I'm a little sceptical of these. It's far simpler just to cut a small square of newspaper and press it onto the surface of the soil; if it soaks up any moisture, don't water the plant. In winter, when plants are semi-dormant, it's far safer to underwater, especially with sensitive souls like *Ficus benjamina* (weeping fig). I water mine once every three weeks and never let any water remain in the saucer – that's guaranteed to send it into a sulk.

There are a couple of other keys to success: feed your plants through the growing season and they'll look much better; secondly, as an extra-special favour, pamper them with some humidity. The atmosphere in most houses is generally quite dry (especially in winter) and while this may suit a few desert plants such as cacti, the vast majority of our houseplants thrive where there is more moisture in the air. Mist them with soft water, group the plants together, or place the pots on saucers of pebbles that are kept damp. Not only will the humid atmosphere improve the health of the plant, it has the added benefit of keeping pests like the dreaded red spider mite away.

If you're still a bit wary of houseplants, build up your confidence by trying some of the plants that I've recommended in my 'Indestructible' list. And occasionally treat yourself to a flowering plant as well – they're usually great value for money, costing the same as, and lasting far longer than, a bunch of flowers. Some of them can live for an amazingly long time, too – I was recently told of a cyclamen that was still going strong and flowering annually after 54 years!

Once you've mastered the art of growing conventional houseplants, it's time to try something more adventurous, like the insect-eating plants (see page 84). One of these, the weirdly beautiful pitcher plant, is the ultimate environmentally friendly fly-catcher, one of the easiest of all plants to grow on a sunny kitchen windowsill and a guaranteed talking point for your visitors. Or what about one of the most choice of plants, a lemon tree? Citrus plants have their own special requirements, but once you've mastered these they're remarkably easy to grow, as I discovered on a visit to Global Orange Groves last summer (page 91).

Having been told that it pays to love and cherish your houseplants, you might be a bit worried about deserting them when you go on holiday. Well, you can now hire the horticultural equivalent of babysitters – but they're a bit pricey, so a few cheaper options for holiday care are discussed on page 81.

Of course, once the houseplant bug really takes hold, you'll start to hanker after a conservatory filled with lush tropical plants. Yet so many of the people who are fortunate enough to own one end up very disappointed with the state of their plants. Anne Swithinbank visited just such a conservatory, and on page 86 she suggests ways of overcoming the problems.

So take a fresh look at your indoor plants. Pamper them as you would a pet, and they'll positively glow with health. And I suppose, when you think about it, they are pretty perfect pets, too; they don't need daily walks, they don't bark when the phone rings, and they'll never bite the postman.

HOUSEPLANTS

Virtually everyone has one houseplant, and some people can even boast quite an extensive collection. But what happens to them when you go on holiday? You may be lucky enough to have a neighbour who is kind enough to plant-sit while you're away, but unless your neighbour has green fingers, your plants may be killed with kindness. However, there are a number of things you can do – with the aid of some common sense and a couple of gadgets – to keep your plants catered for, so follow our basic rules to make sure your house plants are still alive and kicking when you return home.

Holiday survival kit

Make life as stress-free as possible for your plants. If they are on a sunny windowsill or in a brightly lit conservatory, move them to a shadier position. Sunlight will mean they need frequent watering and ventilation to stop them from wilting. If you're not around to do this, your plants will suffer.

Try to group your plants together. Plants release water through their leaves, so by putting them in a group you will increase the humidity and create a small microclimate. Plants will thrive in this humid atmosphere, but make sure you water the pots well before going away.

Check for pests and diseases. If a plant is affected it needs to be treated, otherwise the problem will be far worse, or possibly fatal, by the time you return. Diagnose the cause of the trouble and spray with a suitable fungicide or insecticide. For long-term treatment, use a 'plant pin'. This ingenious technique allows plants to stay trouble-free for weeks at a time. A 'pin' resembling a small plant label is pushed into the compost of the affected plant. This releases an insecticide into the compost, which the plant absorbs.

Remove any flowers, as you don't want plants going to seed while you're away. Any fading blooms could also encourage diseases, so are best cut off.

If you are going away for more than a week, you will have to enlist the help of a neighbour or some self-watering devices. The following should keep your house plants watered for a few weeks:

1. Line a large window box tray or gravel tray with capillary matting. Wet the matting thoroughly and then stand the plants in the tray. The plants will absorb water from the matting.

2. There are many self-watering devices available at garden centres. They all work on the principle of a reservoir of water and a wick. One end of the wick is placed in the water and the other is pushed into the compost. As water is absorbed by the plant, more is carried up the wick from the reservoir, so keeping the compost evenly moist.

3. To make your own self-watering system, take an empty margarine tub, fill it with water, and then replace the lid after cutting a small hole out of it. Take an old pair of tights, cut off one of the legs, and push one end of it through the hole in the margarine lid. Push the other end through the drainage hole in the bottom of the plant pot and stand the plant on top of the margarine tub. Water is then taken up by capillary action into the plant pot. Simple, but very effective.

4. The ultimate technique involves using your toilet. Place the plants in a tray lined with damp capillary matting and stand the whole thing on top of the toilet seat. Run a strip of capillary matting from the cistern down into the tray. Because of the ballcock, the cistern never empties, so your plants will have a constant supply of water. This will keep them happy for weeks.

Another simple method of holiday care for houseplants. Place the plants on a piece of capillary matting on the draining board, with a smaller section of matting used as a wick.

Houseplant questions and answers

I have an African violet (*Saintpaulia*) that hasn't flowered for a long while. What can I do to encourage it to flower?

It's important to make sure that African violets are not too congested in their pots. If the plant looks overcrowded, knock it out of its pot and remove any offsets. Use them as large cuttings, potting them up in a mixture of equal parts sharp sand and compost. Don't cover the cuttings, remember to give them tepid water, and they should soon root. Feed the young plants when they are growing well with half-strength African violet food.

I have a poinsettia which is doing well but is totally green. How do I turn it red again for Christmas?

The bracts that surround the true flowers (which are like yellow beads) will colour as the day length reduces in autumn. If the plant is being grown in a room where there is no artificial light, this should happen automatically. If, however, it's in a room that you use in the evening, you're bound to be switching lights on and off. In this instance, you have to trick the plant. For a period of three weeks it needs to be covered for 16 hours each night with a black polythene bag, spending the remaining eight hours a day in the light. At the end of this treatment, the bracts should start to turn red. It's quite a chore, but it does work.

I have what appear to be hundreds of small black flies coming out from the pots of my houseplants. What are they, and how can I get rid of them?

They are called sciarid flies (or fungus gnat) and it is the larvae that can cause damage – the adult flies are just a nuisance. The flies like wet, almost rotting soil where they can lay the eggs from which the troublesome larvae emerge. Watering the compost at regular intervals with an insecticide should solve this problem. If you would rather not use chemicals, cut fly-paper into strips and hang them among your plants. This will catch the adult flies and stop them from laying eggs.

The red poinsettia, traditionally the most popular houseplant for Christmas.

The African violet (*Saintpaulia*) is one of the best flowering houseplants.

I have grown an avocado plant from a stone and it is now 12 inches/30 cm high. How do I look after it?

Avocado trees (*Persea americana*) are popular plants to grow. The large, egg-like stone within the fruit germinates easily if balanced over a jam-jar of water, with the blunt end just touching the water's surface. A single strong shoot emerges with a cluster of large leaves and at this stage the young plant should be potted up. Avocados are not naturally branching plants, so unless growth is checked they will continue to grow straight up, producing a rather tall, single-stemmed plant. Regularly pinching out the growing point will force it to produce sideshoots, so making a more attractive, bushy plant. Keep your avocado in a warm, light room and in a few years you will have a handsome tree with large, mid-green leaves up to 3 ft/90 cm long.

How do I grow an amaryllis?

Soak the roots of the dried bulb in lukewarm water for a few hours and then pot the bulb in a clay pot, using loam-based compost for extra stability. The pot should be only just wider (about a finger's width) than the bulb, and one-third of the bulb should remain above compost level. Water well and keep in a well-

The avocado is great fun to grow from seed.

lit spot at around 68°F/20°C. It should flower quite happily in a few weeks. When the flowers have faded, cut them off to allow the leaves to develop. Water regularly, add liquid tomato fertilizer once a fortnight and stop watering to give the bulb a rest for three months from mid-summer. Then repot into fresh compost and start again.

Golden rules for houseplants

Many plants can become one-sided or 'facing' plants as they strive to grow towards the light. Turning the plant every couple of weeks (about a quarter turn of the pot each time) will give you a plant with an even shape.

Many houseplants will benefit from a holiday outside in the garden during the warm summer months. Avoid standing them in strong sunlight, as the contrast to the lower light levels in the house could cause leaves to scorch. Stand plants in the shade for a couple of weeks, where they will enjoy the warm summer rains and fresh air.

Plant leaves will quickly collect dust and dirt. Regular cleaning will not only make the plant look cared for but also help the leaves to function properly. There are many products available for cleaning leaves, but don't overdo them – you don't want your plant ending up looking too shiny and plastic. Warm water and a soft cloth will do just as well.

Avoid buying plants that have been outside a shop on a pavement in the winter. While they may initially look healthy, remember that most houseplants have tropical origins and will not take kindly to blasts of cold winter winds. Plants can literally catch a chill, which can result in leaf and flower drop, and even plant death. If you buy plants from a garden centre in winter, make sure they are wrapped well and protected from any sudden temperature changes as you transport them home.

If your houseplant is getting too large and you need to re-pot it, wait until the spring. The plant will then have plenty of time to establish itself before the autumn.

PLANT LIST

Ten indestructible houseplants

Aspidistra elatior (cast-iron plant): An old faithful which survives cold, heat, gas fumes and a degree of neglect.

Chlorophytum comosum (spider plant): A fountain of variegated leaves, plus plantlets on long stems.

Cissus antarctica (kangaroo vine): Stiff, glossy leaves with toothed edges. Quick-growing.

Cyperus (umbrella plant): Stately arching stems topped with leafy umbrellas. Grow in a water-filled pot.

Fatsia japonica: Huge, palmate glossy leaves. Can reach 10 ft/3 m. Pinch out to keep bushy.

Ficus elastica (rubber plant): Large, leathery, oval leaves on a single stiff stem.

Rhoicissus rhomboidea (grape ivy): A bushy climber with pretty, dark green leaves. Vigorous.

Sansevieria trifasciata (mother-in-law's tongue): Tall, fleshy, variegated leaves, tolerates a dry atmosphere.

Schefflera arboricola (umbrella tree): A handsome bushy shrub covered in mid-green glossy 'umbrellas'.

Tradescantia (wandering Jew): Trailing varieties are available in a wide range of colours.

Weird and wonderful

There can be no arguing that carnivorous plants, or insect-eaters, are indeed weird; whether they're wonderful is a matter of personal taste! Like them or loathe them, you cannot help but be intrigued as to how they go about their sinister task, and children are always transfixed.

In their natural habitat insectivorous plants grow in poor, boggy soil. Starved of nutrients, they have had to find other ways of getting food. Slowly, their leaves have developed into a clever means of catching insects, supplying the plants with the nutrients they lack. Once caught, the insects are dissolved and absorbed into the plant's system. The empty insect carcasses serve as a chilling reminder of the efficiency of these bizarre plants.

There are many varied plants that make up this specialized family, but the following are the most commonly grown:

Sundews (*Drosera*) catch prey by using sticky tentacles on long, thin leaves which eventually fold around the victim to hold it in a lethal grip.
Butterworts (*Pinguicula*) use smaller sticky tentacles for trapping, and have broad, flat leaves.
Pitcher plants (*Sarracenia*) have adapted their leaves into tubes or pitchers. Insects are attracted by the sweet nectar secreted at the rim of the tube and, once over the rim, slide on a one-way journey into the bottom of the tube to be absorbed.
The cobra lily (*Darlingtonia californica*) traps insects in the same way.
The Venus fly trap (*Dionaea muscipula*) must be the most ingenious of the carnivorous plants. Many children will have owned one of these plants at some time and been thrilled at watching it literally catch its own lunch. The leaves have developed into green or red traps lined with sensitive hairs. Insects are attracted by nectar in the traps, and when the tiny hairs are triggered as the insect feeds, the traps snap shut. When the insect has been digested the trap reopens, ready to catch its next meal.

A sunny spot is best, and even though they can do well on a windowsill indoors, these plants prefer to be outside in summer, where there will be a plentiful food supply. Sunshine will bring out their colours and encourage them to flower. Water with rain water and stand the plants in saucers to enable you to keep them constantly moist and to increase humidity. Alternatively, stand them in their pots around the edge of a pond during the summer. They will thrive in this moist, humid environment and create a real talking point in your garden.

Right: Surprise your family and friends: pop a pitcher plant in your pond!

CONSERVATORIES

A conservatory should provide the ideal environment for growing the loveliest of plants, from sweet-smelling orange trees to magnificent climbers like the sky-blue plumbago. Yet, sadly, many conservatories are disaster areas for plants because their basic growing needs have been ignored.

Rinske Oerleman thought she had the perfect conditions in her beautiful south-facing conservatory in the Medway Valley. Yet nothing seemed to be thriving, so houseplant expert Anne Swithinbank set out to discover what was going wrong.

ANNE SWITHINBANK:

'As your conservatory faces directly south, it's going to get very hot in summer. The plants inside it will literally cook – they'll get so hot that they won't be able to take up enough water from their roots to make up for all the moisture they're losing through their leaves. This will put your plants under all sorts of stress and will lead to browning leaves and flowers, leaf scorch, and even death.'

RINSKE OERLEMAN:

'Is there anything I can do to prevent this from happening?'

'I've noticed that you haven't any air vents in the roof – that's one of the first things you should think about when planning a conservatory. Hot air rises, and roof vents would allow it to escape. If you have side vents as well, cooler air is drawn in through the sides and escapes through the roof, creating a cooling stream of air. You can't really add vents now, but installing a circulating fan in the roof would be an improvement. It will move the warm air and help cool the conservatory down.

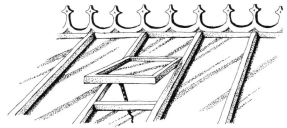

Conservatories need plenty of windows for good ventilation.

'The other thing is blinds. When you think about building a conservatory, include them in your plans right from the start, especially if it is going to be on a west- or south-facing wall. Without the protection of blinds there is not really a lot you can grow apart from cacti and succulents, and even they might start to suffer. Certainly anyone sitting in such a conservatory would find it very hot, bright and uncomfortable.'

'So what sort of plants do you think would do well in a south-facing conservatory?'

'Well, provided you improve the ventilation, add some blinds and make sure the temperature doesn't fall below 50°F [10°C], you can grow a good range of plants. Cordyline australis, or its broader-leaved cousin C. indivisa, both called the cabbage palm, can make a spectacular focal point. Long, green, sword-shaped leaves erupt into a fountain of growth, which eventually forms into a small palm-like trunk. It is very tough and can even grow outside in milder areas. Stand it out on a terrace in the summer, and then move it back into the conservatory for winter.

'Ferns would be ideal to grow under larger plants, in the shade. Blechnum gibbum, with its palm-like crown of stiff fronds, is well suited to a cooler conservatory. It is surprisingly tough and hardy, but must not be subjected to frost.

'The asparagus fern (Asparagus sprengeri), which is not really a true fern, is another good choice for its delicate feathery foliage. Its fleshy roots hold water, so it can tolerate some neglect.

'Clivia miniata (kaffir lily) prefers temperatures a little warmer than the ferns, preferably around 40–45°F [4–7°C]. Given the right conditions, in late winter it will produce clusters of orange flowers held on a robust stem above the thick, dark green, strap-like leaves.'

To make the most of your conservatory:

● Use all the available space to grow plants at different levels – in pots, in beds and in hanging baskets.

● Grow plenty of scented plants like Jasminum polyanthum, whose fragrance will linger in the confined space.

Asparagus densiflorus 'Sprengeri', the virtually indestructible asparagus fern.

Conservatory questions and answers

My stephanotis plant (*Stephanotis floribunda*) has produced a single green fruit, about the size of a duck's egg. How can I tell if it's ripe to pick, as I'd like to sow the seeds?

When the fruit is ripe it will turn yellow and become soft to the touch. This process can take up to a year, with the pod eventually splitting to show plumed seeds. Sow the seeds immediately and, once they have germinated, carefully pot them up into individual pots. Give them bright light, constant temperatures (45–50°F/7–10°C) and keep them pot-bound, and within a few years they should be producing the waxy white, sweetly scented flowers that make this plant a real favourite.

Can you give me some advice on how I can get my *Cymbidium* orchid to flower?

This can be a tricky plant to encourage to flower. Give it a spell outside in spring and summer in a lightly shaded part of the garden. Water moderately, with only half-strength fertilizer, and when spikes start forming in mid-summer stop feeding altogether. In autumn use a high-potash feed to develop the flowers, moving on to a balanced fertilizer in winter. Bring the plant indoors before the first frosts in winter, making sure it is protected from strong sunlight and kept cool. The flamboyant, long-lasting flowers should start to appear during winter and spring. *Phalaenopsis* (moth orchid) is an easy-to-grow alternative to *Cymbidium*, producing lots of open-faced flowers for up to six months of the year.

What better place to relax than in a plant-filled conservatory? However, neither the plants nor you will thrive if the conservatory gets too hot, so make sure you provide sufficient shading and ventilation.

A DOWN-TO-EARTH GUIDE TO ENJOYABLE GARDENING

Golden rules for conservatories

Take the time to think about exactly how you will use your conservatory. Whether it is to be an additional room to the house where plants will take second place or filled to overflowing with tropical foliage, it will need careful planning to incorporate your requirements. Make all your decisions before any building work starts. Try to blend the conservatory with the house, perhaps using the same brick, and bear in mind the need for shading, ventilation, heating and water supply.

If you don't want blinds in your conservatory, train a climbing plant across the inside of the roof to provide important shade. Plants such as the fast-growing passion flower (*Passiflora caerulea*) will soon cover a network of wires and make an attractive but practical canopy.

Most plants thrive in humid conditions, so spray foliage regularly in warm weather with tepid water – but don't do it on sunny days as the leaves may become scorched. Spraying water onto solid floors of ceramic tiles (damping down) will also help.

PLANT LIST

Best conservatory plants

(Assuming moderate temperatures – minimum 55°F/13°C.)

Asplenium nidus (bird's nest fern): Huge shuttlecocks of glossy bright green undivided fronds.

Bougainvillea: A vigorous climber with masses of papery magenta bracts. It needs a sunny position and a hard prune in spring.

Brunfelsia calycina: A shrubby evergreen. Blue flowers fading to white are produced almost all year.

Citrus limon × *sinensis* 'Meyer' (Meyer's Lemon): One of the best citrus plants; small and bushy, with prolific fruits of excellent flavour.

Hoya carnosa: A climber with waxy white flower clusters from spring to autumn. Supremely rich fragrance.

Jasminum polyanthum: A twining climber with clusters of starry white flowers. Very sweet perfume.

Medinilla magnifica: Spectacular pink flowers, borne in heavy clusters beneath wide pink bracts.

Plumbago auriculata: Tall shrubs with glorious powder-blue flowerheads from April to November. It needs support.

Tibouchina urvilleana: An evergreen shrub with large blue-purple satiny flowers from summer to early winter.

Bougainvillea is one of the most reliable and colourful of conservatory plants.

Oranges and lemons

The sweetly-scented flowers and exotic fruits of citrus plants have made them very popular for conservatories. I visited a specialist citrus nursery in Dorset called Global Orange Groves UK and asked owner Patricia Oliver for the secrets of growing perfect oranges and lemons.

PATRICIA OLIVER:

'Most people's first experience of growing citrus is planting an orange pip. These germinate quite easily and grow into bushy plants, but they rarely produce a flower, let alone an orange. Disappointing as this is, don't let it put you off growing citrus. To get a fruiting tree, you need to plant pips of an original variety, like the Seville marmalade orange, rather than a hybrid. Seville will always produce fruit, though it may take five or six years.

'If you want guaranteed fruit, buy a grafted tree. These will flower and fruit continuously in the right conditions. One of the most prolific varieties is a lemon called 'Meyer's Lemon', or 'Four Seasons'. It produces flowers all the time, and fruits as many as four times a year.'

The prolific citrus 'Meyer's Lemon' (*C. limon* × *sinensis* 'Meyer').

RICHARD JACKSON:

'Do citrus make good houseplants?'

'Only smaller varieties like the calamondin orange (Citrus mitis) make good houseplants, though even these need lots of sun and a spell outdoors. Most citrus should really be grown outside, where they will enjoy the fresh air and sun they need. Only bring them into a cool greenhouse or conservatory to protect them from frost in winter. Make sure the temperature doesn't drop too low, as not only will you risk your plants being frosted, but cold conditions will prolong their hibernation and affect their ability to flower.

'In a conservatory, you will be able to give citrus lots of humidity. It's often very difficult to achieve the high humidity level they need in the house. Without it, citrus will often drop their leaves.

'When it comes to repotting, use a lime-free or ericaceous compost, as citrus prefer an acid soil.'

'With any citrus plant that I've grown I've found that after a couple of years it flowers less and less, the leaves start turning yellow, and it hardly produces any fruit. I have fed them regularly but it seems to have little effect. Do they need any special feeding?'

'Feeding is crucial to flowering and fruiting. Many people make the mistake of using a fertilizer with the wrong balance of trace elements, such as liquid tomato food, and feeding in summer only. In fact most citrus fruit in winter, so they need regular feeding all year round. They need a high-nitrogen fertilizer such as Chempak No. 2 in the summer, and a balanced feed – Chempak No. 3, for example – in the winter. If fertilizer is applied weekly, citrus will respond by producing glossy green leaves as well as flowering and fruiting well. At Global Orange Groves, we discovered that citrus need a lot more trace elements than other plants, so we decided to create our own blends of fertilizer – one for winter and one for summer – which we think are the ideal citrus feed. We sell them by mail order from our nursery in Dorset.

'Given constant feeding with the right balance of fertilizer, and put out on a terrace in the summer, citrus are rewarding plants to grow, adding a real touch of the exotic.'

Further details on Global Orange Groves can be found in the list of recommended mail order supplies on page 139.

CHAPTER SIX

THE NATURAL GARDEN

A few years ago, one of the wisest gardeners I've ever known advised me to give up using chemicals in the garden.

'What, not even on the roses?' I responded in panic. 'They'll mutate into greenfly given half a chance.'

'No, leave off the chemicals completely,' he said, 'and your garden will look after itself.'

Well, I took his advice and stopped. In the first season I had palpitations every time I saw a wretched greenfly. But although they did build up on the roses, after a while a miraculous thing happened. They disappeared.

Now, in the second year of the experiment, I've hardly seen a greenfly at all. Nature is balancing itself out, I'm saving a small fortune on chemicals and I've noticed more wildlife visiting. I can't pretend I'm saving the planet, but it's one small step. And I feel pretty good about it all.

Just in case you're thinking I'm sounding a bit smug, I'll own up — I have used chemicals on a couple of occasions to save my hostas. One evening last summer I discovered an army of monster slugs bent on some serious pillage, so I'm afraid I sprinkled a few pellets to stop the invasion. I'd hate to garden without hostas.

Left: A pond creates a wonderful haven for wildlife.

The point I'm making is that I've cut back from over-enthusiastic use of chemicals to virtually no use at all – and I think my garden is the better for it.

I've done one other thing – I've started to build up the soil. The chances are that if you've been adding chemical fertilizers the level of natural soil micro-organisms that promote growth will have gradually declined. To overcome this, add bulky organic compost or well-rotted horse manure – a barrowload per 10–13 ft/3–4 m every year. This way you'll grow stronger plants in healthier soils, and the stronger they are, the more resistant they'll be to potential pests and diseases. It's also worth looking out for disease-resistant varieties of vegetables, roses and fruit to make life even easier.

Another important factor in chemical-free gardening is to grow plenty of annuals with wide-open flowers to attract beneficial insects. The poached egg plant (*Limnanthes*) is worth its weight in gold in any garden for its ease of growth and sheer flower power. Only 6 in/15 cm high, it rockets along the ground producing an abundance of yellow-centred white flowers. Bees love it and, more importantly, so do hoverflies, whose larvae will demolish as many as 50 greenfly each per day. So by encouraging them to visit your garden, you're doing yourself a great favour.

If any plant in your garden is prone to a particular problem, you'll find that there's usually an organic method of dealing with it. Some of the answers to more common problems will be found in Chapter 7, and others can be found in a comprehensive book on organic gardening.

I'm not a zealot about this, and in some instances a chemical solution is preferable. For example, if you do spray your greenfly, ICI Rapid is a far more specific aphid-killer than pyrethrum, which is the blunderbuss organic equivalent. What I'm really asking you to consider is whether you need to spray at all – and if you do, whether a chemical is the best answer. In most instances, it won't be.

I've been delighted by the variety of wildlife that's starting to visit my virtually chemical-free garden and I'm keen to encourage more. I was formerly under the impression that a proper wildlife garden was little more than an overgrown weed patch, teeming with an assortment of horrors like nettles and docks, but in the past year I've met people like Chris Baines (see page 96) who have shown me that it really is surprisingly easy to create a very beautiful wildlife garden.

These wildlife gardeners use good native plants like silver birch and hawthorn, but they don't turn up their noses at foreigners. All the buddleias, for instance, are a magnet for butterflies, and ceanothus will be humming with contented bees. Just about anything that produces fruit or berries is good too – crab apples, cotoneaster, holly, honeysuckle, even ivies. And for the borders they use simple cottage-garden flowers – bluebell, foxglove, forget-me-not, candytuft, snapdragon and hollyhock. A wonderful display, and rich in nectar and pollen.

A pond will add year-round interest, attracting a wide variety of wildlife visitors – especially frogs, which will add their voices to the dawn chorus in spring and (thoughtful of them) catch slugs on the hop. A word of warning, though – don't put goldfish in your pond as they'll eat most of the underwater wildlife, including tadpoles.

Encourage birds into your garden by putting up a nest box.

Birds do such a valuable job mopping up aphids and caterpillars that it's well worth tempting them by providing a bird bath. Chris Baines has designed an ingenious bubbling D-I-Y version and he explains how easy it is to make on page 102. Alternatively, persuade birds to stay by putting up a nest box. Place it in the shade in a sheltered spot, away from bonfires, the prevailing wind and cats. You'll have months of enjoyment watching the birds mark their territories and choose a mate, followed by the frantic domesticity of nest-building and feeding a family.

So, this season, why not create a natural garden? Hang up your spray guns and encourage wildlife to visit, then sit back to watch nature not only enjoying your garden but doing a pretty good job of caring for it as well.

THE NATURAL GARDEN

WILDLIFE IN THE GARDEN

All gardeners can encourage wildlife — even the smallest space, such as a balcony, can be planned to provide food and water for passing birds and butterflies.

With more space, you can add other features. Hedges will provide nesting sites for songbirds, and a pond is a haven for frogs and other visitors. Try to make room for wild flowers too, to add an extra dimension of colour and interest as well as providing a rich habitat for some fascinating and useful insects.

One man in particular, Chris Baines, has pioneered and popularized wildlife gardening. In Hampshire, Chris met fellow enthusiast Wendy Ellicock to see how she had created the perfect haven for wildlife.

An exuberance of natural planting cleverly disguises the edge of this pond.

A DOWN-TO-EARTH GUIDE TO ENJOYABLE GARDENING

CHRIS BAINES:

'One of the loveliest ways to encourage wildlife into the garden is to create a wildflower meadow. Ordinary lawns, while beautiful to the gardener's eye, are a real desert for wildlife – those vast expanses of carpet-like green offer no food, shelter or water. Some people might find it hard to part with their striped lawn, but they only need to sacrifice a small corner to create a beautiful meadow. Yours looks very established.'

WENDY ELLICOCK:

'Well, it didn't happen overnight. A wildflower meadow can take a few years to get going and is a lot of hard work, but it does allow me to grow beautiful native flowers. I find that sowing seeds of wild flowers directly into the meadow is not always successful, with young plants often giving up the struggle to get established. I prefer to sow seeds into trays that have little compartments or plugs. Once they have germinated and grown into small plants, I then prepare an area where I can plant. First strim a small area, about 2–3 ft [60–90 cm] square, then fold back the turf. Pop the young plants out of the trays and plant them in the cleared area. Leave the turf folded back so that they will be able to establish themselves quickly. They should seed and start colonizing that part of the meadow.'

'And once your plants are established, one of the nicest things to do is to collect the seed from your own wildflowers so that you'll be able to propagate more plants to put back into the meadow.

'Late summer is a good time to harvest seeds of plants like cowslips (Primula veris). Wait until the seedheads are ripe – the seeds will often be ready to drop out – then put a paper, not polythene, bag over a whole cluster of seedheads and snap them off. Hang the whole thing up for a week or two, and all the seeds will ripen and drop out into the bag. Sow them immediately while they're very fresh and green, and you will soon be able to fill up your meadow with lots of plants.

'Now that your meadow looks so established, you tell me you're going to cut it all down?'

'Cutting is an essential part of meadow culture, and the end of summer is the ideal time to cut. The flowers will already have seeded themselves and so the whole area can be cut right down. A scythe is fine for this task but I

Wildflower meadows can be colourful and attractive.

prefer to use a strimmer, which gets the job done much quicker.'

'You're presumably cutting it, then raking it all off?'

'Yes, it's important to rake it off as otherwise the grass cuttings will break down and put nutrients back into the soil. This is quite the opposite of conventional gardening, where you are trying to build up nutrient levels all the time, but is essential if you want a thriving wildflower meadow. One of the problems of a meadow is that grasses like good soil, while the flowers thrive on poor soil. So if you don't want the grasses to take over and smother the flowers, rake the grass cuttings off and keep the nutrient levels low.'

'Not everybody will be able to cope with long grass and a meadow in their garden, but anyone who's interested in wildlife has to begin with a pond. Yours is magnificent. Is it natural?'

'No, it's entirely artificial. As we wanted quite a large pond, we had a digger in for three days to do all the hard work. The driver was given very careful instructions as to where to make shallow edges and where to build shelves.'

'Gently shelving sides are so important. They allow creatures like frogs to get in and out, make a place for dragonflies to lay their eggs and provide perfect growing conditions for the many wildflowers which enjoy wet feet.'

'We purposely built the pond right outside the house so that we could watch the enormous amount of wildlife that it attracts. We are particularly lucky in that we even have a resident kingfisher.'

Wendy Ellicock built her pond close to the house so that she could easily observe all the wildlife it attracts.

A DOWN-TO-EARTH GUIDE TO ENJOYABLE GARDENING

Dragonflies are one of the most popular pond visitors.

'With terms like greenhouse effect and ozone layer becoming part of our language, people are now beginning to realize that they should start doing their little bit to help. And there's so much you can do if you have a garden, no matter what the size.

'Wildflower meadows and ponds are great wildlife magnets, but what if you don't want your garden to look like some sort of nature reserve?'

'Wild doesn't necessarily mean overgrown. If you don't want a wild garden, use native English plant varieties, as well as lots of cottage-type plants, like lavender, which is always popular with bees, and plants that produce berries, like cotoneaster. The basic rule is to plant anything that will attract wildlife.

The reliable, colourful and fast-growing *Lavatera olbia* 'Rosea'.

Wildlife questions and answers

What plants would you recommend to make up a good wildlife hedge?

The idea is to give as much variety as possible, as well as food and shelter all year round. Elder (*Sambucus*) is a valuable hedgerow plant with white flowers in spring followed by rich, dark berries in late summer. Hawthorn (*Crataegus*) will create the perfect nesting site, with a dense network of branches. Dog roses (*Rosa canina*) with their simple pale pink flowers and colourful autumn hips must be included, as well as wild clematis, or old man's beard (*Clematis vitalba*), which has scrambling stems covered in distinctive fluffy seedheads in autumn. Even oak and beech can be grown in a hedge, and can be kept under control with an annual trim. However, where space allows, let the plants grow wild so that they will be able to produce their valuable flowers and berries freely.

I have a buddleia bush in my garden and I'm thrilled at the number of butterflies it has attracted. Are there any other plants that butterflies love?

The nectar of the sunflower is a favourite of butterflies (and sunflower seeds are always popular with birds). Honesty (*Lunaria annua*), more commonly known for its silver seed cases, is a good butterfly plant for early in the season. Its purple flowers attract many species, and to some this plant is an excellent food source for their caterpillars. Towards the end of the season, *Sedum spectabile* (ice plant) is a valuable source of nectar when many other plants have long since finished flowering. The large plate-like clusters of

pink flowers make great landing pads for hungry butterflies. But one plant that rivals even the buddleia for popularity with butterflies is the humble mint. It is one of the best butterfly plants around, and is so easy to grow.

Frogs are one of the best allies in the fight against slugs.

I have just made a wildlife pond, and would like some frogs in it. Where can I get them from?

There is no point in putting adult frogs into your pond, hoping they will stay. Many amphibians, including frogs, have a strong homing instinct, and will return to the pond where they were born when the breeding season comes around. You will have much more success if you introduce some frog spawn instead. Find a friend or neighbour whose pond is overpopulated and remove the spawn while it is still fresh. As long as your pond is full of plant and animal life, the emerging tadpoles shouldn't need feeding.

'For me, the mallow (Lavatera olbia) *is the perfect plant for insects. It produces lots of open flowers that allow insects easy access to the nectar and pollen. The secret is to make sure that there's a constant supply of pollen and nectar right through the year.'*

'And what about shelter and nesting sites?'

'Well, I think it's also important to cover the surface of the ground or flower border so that there is plenty of good ground cover to provide hiding places. Allow plants to grow up the side of the house to make nesting sites for birds and aim to create a garden that will give food, shelter and water. Try to bring the whole thing together so that it really is a garden, while providing a variety of habitats for the local wildlife.'

'And even if you've only got a balcony, you can grow plants in pots and hanging baskets and still pull in the wildlife.'

Golden rules for wildlife gardens

Although it's very tempting to keep the garden as tidy as possible, don't be too keen to cut plants down after they have flowered – leave them to develop seedheads which will provide food for many species of bird. The dead foliage will also provide shelter for many animals during the winter months.

If you want to let your lawn grow into a wildflower meadow but are worried that it will look a mess, keep the perimeter of the lawn regularly mown, and perhaps also cut a path through the middle. This will make your uncut meadow look much more purposeful, and not as though you've forgotten to get the mower out!

A wildflower meadow provides a natural boundary to a lawn.

PLANT LISTS

Best ornamental plants for attracting wildlife

Trees

Betula pendula (silver birch): A lovely, white-stemmed tree, attracting over 200 insect species.

Crataegus (hawthorn): An excellent hedge plant that provides berries, insects, shelter and nest-sites for birds.

Sorbus aucuparia (rowan): A graceful tree with flowers for the bees and berries for the birds.

Shrubs

Buddleia: All varieties act as a magnet for butterflies, bees and a host of other insects.

Cotoneaster: Blackbirds, robins and thrushes are among the many birds which enjoy the berries.

Lavandula (lavender): A superb butterfly and bee plant.

Pyracantha: A handsome shrub with a reliably heavy crop of berries for birds.

Herbaceous perennials

Centranthus ruber (valerian): Showy red flower spikes which attract a huge number of insects.

Phlox paniculata: The strongly perfumed flowers are especially attractive to butterflies and moths.

Sedum spectabile 'Autumn Joy': Provides late summer nectar for butterflies and winter seed for birds.

Ten annuals to attract hoverflies

Borago officinales (borage): Small starry flowers of clear blue. Can also be used to add some colour and interest to your salads and drinks.

Calendula officinalis (pot marigold): Bright orange or yellow flowers all summer.

Cosmos bipinnatus: Filmy foliage, large daisy flowers on tall stems. Good colour range.

Erysimum cheiri (wallflower): Showy spring flowers, with some superb single colours.

Eschscholzia californica (Californian poppy): Generally orange-yellow, though lovely colour mixes are available.

Helianthus annuus (sunflower): Giant plants which are great fun to grow. Dwarf varieties are also available.

Iberis umbellata (candytuft): Pretty posies of flowers in all shades from white to carmine.

Limnanthes douglassii (poached egg plant): Quick-growing, free-seeding and the best of all if you're a hoverfly.

Lobularia maritima (alyssum): A traditional edging plant, forming neat white or pink cushions.

Myosotis alpestris (forget-me-not): Piercingly blue flowers, self-seeds very readily. It's actually a biennial, but who's counting?

Avoid having bonfires as they pollute the air. Many of the things you would normally burn can actually be composted or, alternatively, put through a shredder (which can easily be hired for a day) and then used for composting or mulch.

Avoid using chemicals, however bad you think a pest problem is. If you encourage birds into the garden they will deal with the majority of pests, and the rest you will just have to learn to live with. The benefits will far outweigh the problems as you discover a new world of wildlife in your garden, and you'll be creating a healthier environment, too.

Water is essential in a wildlife garden, but it can be a deathtrap to smaller mammals. Hedgehogs can easily fall into a pond while having a drink, and unless they have some means of getting out they will soon tire and drown. Create a shallow end in your pond, perhaps leading into a marshy area where an animal will be able to climb out. Alternatively, lay a large branch in the water or make a wooden ramp leading up out of the pond as an escape route.

Ponds and bird baths

No wildlife garden could ever be complete without the addition of a water environment. With the continued destruction of wetland habitats in our countryside, back-garden ponds (see page 27) have become increasingly important. These urban oases have been a lifeline for the common frog, which might otherwise have become extinct by now. Countless other creatures like pondskaters and dragonflies will soon make a pond their home, and there will be more that will come to drink and bathe in the water.

The Bubbling Bird Bath makes an attractive feature when sunk into the garden. Being shallow, small animals like hedgehogs can drink safely from it without danger of drowning, and birds will flock to enjoy a bath or a drink.

But not everyone has the space available to create as large a pond as Wendy did in her wildlife garden and people with young children are obviously concerned about safety. However, this shouldn't stop you creating something relatively cheap, safe and attractive. When challenged with this problem, wildlife expert Chris Baines came up with an ingenious solution – the Bubbling Bird Bath. This shallow water feature is safe for children, while providing a place for hedgehogs to drink and birds to bathe.

In the following pictures, Chris shows you just how easy and simple it is to make – in fact, he made his in only a few hours.

Materials

1 plastic dustbin
1 small submersible pump
1 4-ft/1.2-m length of hosepipe
1 shallow terracotta bowl
small amount of mastic
pebbles

Carefully cut a plastic dustbin in half, taking care that the cut is level. This will make the base of the Bubbling Bird Bath.

Half-fill the dustbin with water and place a small submersible pump in the bottom, with approximately 4 ft/1.2 m of hosepipe attached.

Take the dustbin lid and make three holes, one in the middle, which should be large enough for the hosepipe to go through, and two more either side. These are necessary in order to allow the water to drain back into the reservoir in the dustbin.

Place a shallow terracotta bowl on the upturned lid, and thread the hosepipe up through the middle hole of the lid and then through the bowl. Cut off the hosepipe to length, and seal around the base of the pot with mastic to prevent any water leakage. Fill the bowl and lid with pebbles.

Turn the pump on and adjust it so that the water gently bubbles over the rim of the bowl, draining back into the dustbin below.

CHAPTER SEVEN

BEATING

THE PROBLEMS

Over the past couple of years, while I struggled to contain invading hordes of slugs and snails, Esther Rantzen and Desmond Wilcox had a far greater worry. Their garden in the New Forest was besieged with rabbits and the little devils had munched their way through the herb bed, graduated to the roses and polished off the shrubs as dessert.

Rather than saying 'That's life', the couple noticed that certain plants, like foxgloves and the old-fashioned roses, were being ignored, so they brought in more of these rabbit-resistant varieties and stopped bothering to plant anything that the rabbits obviously adored. In addition, they put up temporary fences at night and whenever they were away on holiday. This helped the young plants get to the stage where they were large enough to be virtually rabbit-proof.

So, despite the odds, Esther and Desmond have managed to establish a pretty cottage garden. They didn't allow themselves to be beaten by the problem; instead, they adapted their gardening methods in order to cope with it.

Lateral thinking also helps with the town gardener's main menace, next door's cats. Rather than trying to put them off with a battery of expensive deterrents, just do the complete opposite. Plant something quite

Left: The sight every gardener dreads – greenfly on the roses.

105

irresistible, like catmint, in a part of the garden where they can do no harm at all and, with any luck, they will ignore everything else.

However, the owners of a garden in Ringwood that I visited were driven to distraction by all the local cats and the only obvious solution was to use a deterrent. But which one? To find out, we set up a trial of everything from sonic devices to gooey substances smelling of cheap aftershave. We even tried lion manure, though it has to be said it wasn't a roaring success. The products that stood the test of time were Get Off spray and Pepper Dust. I suspect, though, that in the long term the best answer would be to have a dog!

It almost comes as a relief to deal with the more readily controllable pests, such as slugs, snails and greenfly. I have some friends who are obsessed by slugs. Every evening after supper they patrol their garden by torchlight, popping any culprits into a bucket of salt water. They even keep a log and their record, I was horrified to hear, was over 1,500 in two weeks.

I'm far too squeamish for the salt-water treatment, preferring to despatch my slugs in an alcoholic haze (them, not me) by using beer traps. The slugs are attracted by the smell and fall in and drown (presumably very happily). And in case you're wondering which beer to use, an eccentric scientist tested out bitter, lager, non-alcoholic lager and stout. Amazingly, the non-alcoholic lager worked best!

Frogs are by far the preferred solution, if you have a pond. Just import a few tadpoles and you'll soon have a flourishing population, slugging it out with the local gastropods. However, it's still worth taking precautions with really vulnerable young plants like delphiniums by surrounding them with a circle of grit. Slugs will refuse to crawl over it, however tempting the treat growing inside.

As discussed in Chapter 6, greenfly can be controlled by natural predators like hoverflies, so grow flowers such as the poached egg plant (*Limnanthes douglasii*) to attract them. Of course, the other thing about greenfly is that it's so easy to squirt them off with an accurately-aimed blast of water from the hosepipe. With any luck, you could turn this into a game for the kids!

In the USA you can buy jam-jars of ladybirds to unleash on your hapless greenfly. I haven't as yet seen them on sale in the UK, but plenty of other biological controls are now widely available to banish virtually all greenhouse and conservatory pests. Most can be bought at garden centres, and are extremely effective.

The control of diseases isn't necessarily a matter of reaching for the spray gun either. Powdery mildew, for instance, flourishes in hot, dry conditions, so good watering and mulching will minimize the possibility of attack. Vigilance helps, too, so if you see an affected leaf, whip it off immediately before the disease can spread. And at the end of the year, tidy up well, gather up any rotting or diseased plant material and burn it or take it to the dump. But in the last resort, if you do have to spray, follow Pippa Greenwood's sensible safety advice on page 108.

It's worth reiterating that beating the weeds is nowhere near the chore you might imagine. Fair enough, you first have to get rid of the perennial weeds – by digging or spraying or covering with polythene for a year – but from then on it's easy. Fight them with plants and mulches. Anna Pavord takes up arms on page 114.

And finally, if you really want the ultimate revenge on your garden problems, you could eat them. No, I'm not talking about the cats – rather, some of the weeds like chickweed and young dandelion leaves which can be delicious in salads. And I've even got a copy of a Victorian booklet called *Why Not Eat Insects?* Do get in touch if you'd like a recipe for Boiled Cod and Snail Sauce, or Braised Beef with Caterpillars.

PESTS AND DISEASES

All gardeners have their share of gardening problems, many of which will be the result of pests or diseases. How do you pick the right product, organic or chemical, when there are so many to choose from?

One of the country's leading experts on pests and diseases is Pippa Greenwood, who works for the Royal Horticultural Society. She offered some advice on choosing and using the best solution:

Another all too common sight – blackspot on roses.

PIPPA GREENWOOD:

'If you think there's something wrong with a plant, the first thing to do is to identify the problem correctly. Some will have easy-to-spot symptoms, while others can be more difficult. It is worth consulting a good book to help you pinpoint the problem exactly, as only then will you be able to treat it.

'Look closely at the plant. If you see something rushing around munching holes out of the leaves, then you obviously have a pest problem. Diseases can be a little more difficult to spot, but your plant should show some sort of visible outward signs – perhaps a white fungus on the leaves, or lumps appearing on the stems. Such symptoms should be relatively easy to look up in a book and identify. Then it's down to the garden centre to buy the right product – but there is such a bewildering range that choosing the right one can become something of a nightmare.

'First take a good hard look at the packet – it should tell you quite clearly what sort of plants you can use it on, and any precautions that you need to take. It will also say exactly which pests it will control.

'Insecticides fall into two groups, contact insecticides and systemic insecticides. The former will only kill off the pest if they come into direct contact with it, so spraying needs to be very accurate and thorough. If the pest is small and hides under a leaf or branch there is every chance that you'll miss it when you spray, so leaving it free to carry on attacking your plant.

'When you spray or water a plant with a systemic product, the insecticide is absorbed into the plant and carried in its sap. When the pest puts its mouth-parts into the plant to feed, it gets a mouthful of insecticide and is killed. Even if you only spray a part of the plant the insecticide is taken into the whole plant, so any pests on distant branches should still be affected. This type of insecticide is particularly useful for taller plants that you might have difficulty spraying all over, or ones with very tightly curled leaves where the chemical won't be able to penetrate.

'If you have more than one problem, such as pests plus a disease, buy one of the products with a good mix of insecticide and fungicide. For example, a rose bush may be affected by aphids and black spot, for which you can buy a product that tackles both at one go.

'People are often worried about using chemicals on things they are going to eat, and quite rightly so. Using the wrong product is potentially dangerous. If you need to spray anything edible, like fruit or vegetables, check the back of the packet carefully. The instructions will tell you whether that product can be used on edible crops, and it will also state the harvest interval – that is, the amount of time you have to wait after spraying before you can pick and eat your plants.

'Safety is something that always worries gardeners, and we'd be very short-sighted if it didn't. Occasionally, at a garden centre or nursery, you may see the staff doing some spraying dressed in all manner of protective clothing, with boots, face mask, gloves and plastic suit.

'This really is only for the professionals, who will be using stronger chemicals than the average gardener. You certainly won't have to wear protective clothing to use any chemicals that you can buy at a garden centre.

Protective clothing is usually worn by professional gardeners when spraying chemicals.

'Always follow the instructions on the packet very carefully, making sure you measure out the correct quantities – many products come with a little measuring cap, which is very useful. Then it's simply a question of pouring the chemical into a sprayer or watering can, topping up with the right amount of water, and away you go.

This attack of blackspot is bad enough to justify spraying. Left unattended, the problem will rapidly get worse.

'However, before you spray, ask yourself if it's really necessary. Gardeners can be a hypercritical lot, but if the plant is not suffering too much, and is not covered in unsightly blotches, why not leave it well alone?'

Pests and diseases questions and answers

Why have my young tomato plants got small white spots on their leaves?

They are suffering from an insect called leaf hopper. After this insect has fed, it removes its mouthparts from the leaf and leaves a pin-prick sized white mark. It is very common and can affect any tomato variety. Use a systemic insecticide.

How do I deal with woolly aphid on my apple tree?

The woolly coating protects this pest, so you will have to use an insecticide. An alternative would be to get up into the tree with some soapy water, and literally wash it all off.

My basil plant (*Ocimum basilicum*) is being attacked by aphids. How do I get rid of them?

Aphids tend to go for young shoots, so nip out the tips of plants to avoid aphid attack. Alternatively, buy a soap-based spray, such as Phostrogen's Safer range.

I have a cherry tree whose leaves seem to be growing with distorted tips. What is wrong?

It is suffering from blackfly, which is causing the leaf distortion. Spray with a jet of water to wash them off, or with a soap-based spray. If you have to use chemicals, use Rapid, which only affects greenfly and blackfly and will not harm beneficial insects. Follow the instructions carefully, and don't spray when it is windy. Of course, the easiest way is to squash them between your finger and thumb, but this is not for the squeamish!

What is causing the knobbly growths on the root of my cherry tree?

It is crown gall, which results from a bacterial infection getting into the plant through a wound, often at ground level. It can affect apple and plum trees, and flowering cherry, too. Treatment is rarely necessary but, if the infection is very bad, remove the plant and dig lots of organic matter into the hole before replanting.

How do I get rid of ants?

If they are in the house sprinkle talcum powder where they run, as they don't like walking on it! In the garden you can use one of the many ant killers on the market, but as ants can be beneficial it is best to leave them well alone if you can tolerate them.

Is there an effective treatment for lily beetle?

Originating in the Surrey area, and now spreading rapidly through the country, this easy-to-spot red beetle can strip lily plants in a few days. The most effective course of action is to watch your lily plants closely, and at the first signs of attack, pick off the beetle – and its muddy-coloured larvae, which live on the underside of the leaves – and squash it. Simple but effective!

I am fighting a losing battle with moles, which are rampaging across my lawn. How can I get rid of them without using traps?

Moles are very sensitive to noise, so put something like a musical birthday card in one of the mounds. It will play for around three days, and the noise will drive them away. For more persistent moles, exchange the card for a small radio playing Radio 1. Amazingly enough, it really does work.

Banish them by playing 'Mole of Kintyre' on your radio!

What is causing mildew on my climbing roses?

Mildew appears when there is poor air circulation, so keep the roses pruned every year so that they don't

An unsightly attack of mildew on roses.

become congested. Dryness at the roots also encourages mildew, so keep the plants well watered, especially if they are growing against a house wall, and spray with a fungicide such as Benlate or Nimrod-T. This fungus can be harboured in the rose leaves, so in the autumn make sure you clear them all away.

My chrysanthemums are being attacked by white rust. How do I treat them?

The buff-coloured warty lumps of white rust will make the leaves curl up and can actually kill the plant. Try to improve the air circulation around the plants, and spray three times at weekly intervals with double-strength Tumbleblite.

What is wrong with my peony, which has grey-brown patches all over it?

It is suffering from grey mould. The best treatment is to remove those parts with the mould on and then replant the peony in a more open, sunnier spot. Remember not to plant it too deeply or it might stop flowering.

The ugly effects of peach leaf curl.

I have a dwarf peach whose leaves curl up and go brown with red blisters. What is causing this?

This is peach leaf curl; you need to spray the tree with a copper fungicide before the tree comes into blossom and leaf, and then again after the leaves have dropped in autumn. A polythene lean-to canopy from mid-winter for six months can help to prevent this disfiguring problem. Leave the ends of the canopy open to allow for ventilation and access by pollinating insects.

Can you tell me what the fluffy brown stuff growing on the back of my hebe leaves is?

This is downy mildew, which will make the leaves turn yellow and develop ugly brown patches. Spray with a fungicide specifically for this sort of mildew, such as Dithane.

Why are my young cabbage plants stunted?

This is one of the signs of club root, which can attack any brassica. Older plants will produce discoloured leaves and wilt on hot days. It is best to burn diseased plants and to dip the roots in a fungicide when planting seedlings. Mulching with manure will reduce the risk of infection, but as this is a soil-borne problem, it might be best to move your brassicas to a fresh patch in the garden.

Can you tell me why my apples have cork-like marks on them?

This is apple scab, caused by a fungus which occurs in damp weather. It marks the apples but they can still be eaten, provided they are peeled first. Make sure you prune out dead or crossed growth, and treat the tree with a tar oil water wash in winter. Spray fortnightly from bud burst in spring with Benlate, and your tree should improve.

The leaves on my roses seem to be rolling up. Can you tell me what is causing this?

They are under attack from an insect called sawfly. The leaves are protecting the small green larvae inside the roll. Ignore it if it is a minor attack, otherwise spray with Sybol.

I'm keen to use biological control methods in my greenhouse, but where can I buy them from?

Many larger garden centres offer a mail-order facility; or look in the classified advertisements of a gardening magazine.

Leaf-rolling sawfly causes this curious curling of rose leaves.

Golden rules for chemicals

Chemicals should always be treated with respect. Read and follow the instructions with great care. Make sure you are using the right chemical for the right job, and that you have diluted it correctly.

Store your garden chemicals safely. Keep them well out of the reach of young children, preferably in a locked cupboard.

Throw away any products that lose their labels, or where the label becomes illegible. Keep them in their original container. It is particularly important that you don't store chemicals in an old drinks bottle, or anything similar.

Try to make up just enough solution for the job in hand. Any that's left over should not be kept. Don't tip it down the kitchen sink or toilet (where it could contaminate the water supply), but pour onto an area of uncultivated ground. These products are designed to be biodegradeable, so will break down and become harmless over a period of time. For larger quantities, contact the Waste Disposal Department of your local council, who may be able to arrange a collection. Alternatively, take them to a local authority refuse disposal site.

Always wash your equipment out thoroughly after you have finished in order to remove all traces of the chemical. It's a good idea to keep a watering can and sprayer especially for chemicals. Mark them very clearly.

When spraying houseplants indoors, make sure you open a window for ventilation. If the weather is warm, dry and calm, it would be better to take your plants outside where you can give them a thorough spray.

Take particular care when using chemicals near a pond, or indoor fish tank. Any careless spraying could contaminate the water and have lethal consequences for its inhabitants.

WEEDS

Weeding is one of the most unpopular, boring and time-consuming jobs in the garden. It's also one of those jobs that gets harder the longer you put it off, especially if you let the weeds produce seed which will plague you for up to seven years. However, it is possible to minimize the chore, first by getting rid of as much perennial weed as possible and then by using ground-cover plants, mulches or weedkillers to control the rest.

Gardening writer Anna Pavord visited Canon David Marriott to help him fight the good fight against weeds

Pea shingle, laid over plastic, makes an attractive weed suppressant.

ANNA PAVORD:

'Weeds can be an annual problem for everyone, and the sooner you deal with them the better. But before you reach for the chemicals, there are alternative ways to keep weeds under control. For a start, there are mulches. Have you ever used mulches before?'

CANON DAVID MARRIOTT:

'No, I haven't. What are they, and how do they work?'

'A mulch is usually a layer of organic material that is put over a border. If you put it on thick enough – which is at least 2–3 inches [5–7 cm] thick – you can actually drown the weeds and prevent them from coming up. But before you put the mulch down, you have to do a bit of groundwork first.

'It is wise to get rid of all the weeds in the area you are going to mulch first. Pull them out by hand, trying to remove as much, if not all, of the weed's roots as well. Alternatively, hoe all the weeds down. Try to choose a sunny, breezy day for this job, as the heat and wind will dry the weeds out and kill them faster. Hoeing on a damp day will usually mean that the weeds are not completely killed, in which case they can quickly reroot and start growing again.

'Once your area is clear of weeds, you can put a mulch down. They come in various forms. There is spent mushroom compost, which is pleasant to work with and looks attractive when covering a border; bark chippings, which are quite effective, but can be expensive and look a little coarse; cocoa-shell, a by-product from the chocolate industry, which is also quite expensive and may need damping down initially to stop it blowing away; garden compost and manure, both cheaper alternatives, but you will need a large quantity and both may carry weed seeds; grass cuttings – something everyone has plenty of, but they are not very attractive so are best used around fruit trees or in the vegetable patch; and gravel, which looks very attractive but is perfect for annual weeds to seed in too, so will need some weeding.

'Newspaper is also an effective mulch if you put lots of layers down and then damp it down with some water. But it's unsightly, so it's best used as a barrier to weeds under a covering of soil or a layer of a more attractive mulch.'

'But once I've put the mulch down, won't it be difficult to water the plants properly with all that mulch in the way?'

Shredded bark conserves moisture and helps keep weeds at bay.

'That's the other good thing about mulches. They actually lock water into the bed, keeping the ground underneath nice and moist, so you don't have to keep going around watering your borders.'

'Well, I'm all for that, but it does mean that the beds will look more like a lot of mulch rather than plants. Isn't there anything else you can do?'

'Once you have got rid of your weeds, you can plant something else in their place, which will smother out the weeds, and there'll be no space for them to grow again.'

'Have you any plants you can recommend?'

'I have three particular favourites that do this job very well. Alchemilla mollis (lady's mantle) is a perennial that forms a clump of round, pale green leaves with crinkled edges. In mid-summer it freely produces lovely lime-green flowers and seeds itself easily. Epimedium × rubrum (bishop's hat) is a perennial which forms a carpet of heart-shaped green leaves that become tinged with brownish-red in the winter, with odd mitre-shaped flowers

The pretty foliage of ground-cover plant *Epimedium* × *rubrum*.

Alchemilla mollis is a particularly attractive and versatile ground-cover plant.

in spring. Galeobdolon argentatum *(syn. Lamium galeobdolon 'Variegatum') is the offputting name for a plant that can cover a large area. It's a perennial that forms a carpet of silver and grey-green nettle-like foliage, with small, tubular, lemon-coloured flowers appearing in summer. This plant can become a little too good at its job and start smothering every other plant in your border, so it may need to be kept in check.'*

'That's fine in a border, but what about the hundreds of weeds coming up in between the bricks in my terrace?'

'Well, I'm afraid that there are some weeds that can't be tackled without using weedkillers (herbicides). Just as with pest and disease problems, it's vital to choose the right weedkiller for the right job. I try not to use weedkillers that are residual. This means a weedkiller that carries on working in the soil for weeks or even years, and while there a few instances where I think their use is justified, I would rather not use them at all.

'Weedkillers fall into two groups: selective and non-selective. Selective weedkillers are used on a limited group of plants – for example, where the garden plants are resistant to the weedkiller, but the targeted weeds are not. A good example is a lawn weedkiller. Non-selective weedkillers will damage garden plants as well as weeds, so have to be used carefully.

'Weedkillers come in various forms: they can be applied through the leaves, where they are absorbed into the plant's system, killing it from inside; they can be used as a short-lived contact spray, where they kill only those parts of the plant they touch; or they can be watered on to the soil, where they are absorbed through the plant's roots, killing it from inside.

'When you've decided what weedkiller to use, follow the instructions on the packet carefully – they are there for a reason! Mix up the exact quantities and don't be tempted to mix it up double-strength thinking that it will work twice as well; in fact it will work only half as well, because you have interfered with the amounts. And if the instructions tell you to use a sprinkle bar, don't just go and slosh it on – do use a sprinkle bar.'

'Does it matter what the weather's like when you put weedkillers on?'

'It can be crucial to you getting the weedkiller in the right or wrong place, particularly if you are spraying. Choose a still, calm day, otherwise your spray could easily be blown across the garden and damage other plants.'

Golden rules for weeding

Never let weeds go to seed. The old adage 'One year's seed equals seven years' weeds' is, unfortunately, only too true.

One of the most effective and satisfying methods of controlling weeds is to hoe them regularly. This is best done on a sunny day, so that the weeds shrivel up in the heat.

If perennial weeds are creeping under your fence from next door's garden, it may be worth digging a trench 12 inches/30 cm deep and lining the side with sturdy polythene. This should act as a barrier to any further invasions.

Bark mulches look good, but can be very expensive – a 4-inch/10-cm layer costs around £6 a square yard/square metre. Halve the cost by putting layers of newspaper down first, and then cover this with just 2 inches/5 cm of bark. This works just as effectively.

Weeding questions and answers

How can I get rid of creeping cinquefoil?

This weed with small strawberry-like leaves and yellow flowers spreads by means of runners. It can colonize 12 sq yd/10 sq m in one season, so you need to keep it under control. Dig it out regularly, especially if it's among other plants, or use a systemic weedkiller.

I have a problem with grass growing in between my slab path. I don't really want to use a chemical, so is there something else you can recommend?

Bio Speedweed is a soap-based product, similar in principle to those that Victorian gardeners would have used, which dehydrates the plant. As it is soap-based, it is harmless to children and animals. It also foams up when used, so you can easily see where you have sprayed. It comes in a ready-to-use pack, complete with sprayer. However, it is rather expensive. It works better on annual weeds rather than perennials.

I have thistles invading my garden from a neighbouring field, and have great problems getting rid of them. Have you any suggestions?

The perennial thistle is difficult to eradicate in one go. Try to dig out as many as possible, but undoubtedly some small pieces of root will be left in the ground. These will appear a few weeks later, and will have to be dug out as well. Alternatively, a couple of applications of Tumbleweed will work effectively.

Help! Japanese knot weed is taking over my garden. What can I do?

It's very difficult to get rid of this invasive plant. It can even grow through walls and tarmac, and can easily take over the whole garden unless you control it by hoeing constantly and pulling it out. When the plant gets bigger, snap it in half, and carefully pour a weedkiller down the hollow stem. Whatever you do, do not allow it to seed.

Mind-your-own-business (*Helxine soleirolii*) is taking over my lawn.

Use a selective or spot lawn weedkiller. This plant often grows under glasshouse staging, where it thrives in moist conditions. Its creeping habit makes it rather invasive, and it can often end up in unwanted places. Incidentally, it has changed its name to *Soleirolia soleirolii* – but a name change doesn't make it any more appealing.

Is there something I could put under shingle or gravel to stop weeds?

Use plastic membrane, which is available in rolls. It forms a barrier to weeds, while still allowing rain to get through to the soil underneath. Always bed such material on a flat surface.

Can you tell me how to deal with bindweed?

It's very difficult to eliminate bindweed from a garden. Drastic measures are needed, which can involve removing plants from a border and digging out all the weed, especially its roots. You can paint the leaves with a glyphosate-based weedkiller, but it will take a number of applications to have any effect. Alternatively, dip the end of the stems in a jam-jar containing Tumbleweed.

Make sure you deal with bindweed quickly before it takes over the entire garden.

How can I get rid of mare's tail?

This prehistoric weed needs severe treatment. The current advice is to bruise the plant by treading on it before applying a weedkiller with glyphosate, such as Round Up or Tumbleweed. The theory is that the weedkiller has a faster effect through the bruised stems. It will need a couple of applications. Alternatively, smother it with black polythene for a year – but obviously this is only possible in certain less prominents parts of the garden.

CHAPTER EIGHT

PRACTICAL SKILLS

During the course of filming the *Grass Roots* series, we answered thousands of questions on every aspect of gardening. Some of the practical questions have cropped up so regularly that I felt I should devote a small section to these specific skills.

One of the easiest, and certainly cheapest, methods of getting new plants is to take cuttings. Sadly, many people don't bother because they're baffled by all the different techniques that are used. On page 120, Sue Phillips demystifies the whole subject.

Earlier in the book I discussed the benefits of growing trained fruit, especially cordons. To get the best crop, it's important to prune fruit trees every summer. Luckily it's not as complicated as you might think, as Matthew Biggs explains on page 125.

I'm a great enthusiast for growing plants from seed. Every year I experiment with new varieties, sometimes to be disappointed, but more often to be delighted — and to me that's all part of the fun of gardening. Some varieties need pampering but I prefer ones such as hardy annuals, which are remarkably easy to grow. Discover how on page 123.

As a gardener, I much prefer hedges to fences. They're far simpler to care for and they look so much prettier, especially if they're kept in trim. Our brief

Left: Well-maintained hedges at Great Dixter.

guide to hedges on page 130 explains this further.

Potential flower-arrangers will enjoy the special section (page 130) on the flowers and foliage that appeal to gardeners and arrangers alike. And, to finish on a more controversial note, I suggest how to care for your lawn – as little as possible!

CUTTINGS

Ripe, semi-ripe, heels and layers – all ways of getting new plants from your old ones. Is it complicated and confusing, or is it an easy way of getting something for nothing? Gardening writer and broadcaster Sue Phillips is an expert at propagating, and she set John Hirst of Kent off on the right lines.

John had an existing shrub border which he wanted to duplicate on the other side of his garden. With limited finances, cuttings from the existing shrubs were the answer. Cuttings can be taken right through the summer, when plenty of young, new shoots are available.

SUE PHILLIPS:

'You've got a nice hardy hibiscus. How do you fancy a few more of those in your new border? I would take young shoots that have grown this year and tear them off from the bottom, so that there's a little bit of old wood with them. They should be kept as fresh as possible, so the trick is to pop them into plastic bags while you're collecting the other cuttings.'

JOHN HIRST:

'Can I take cuttings from my hydrangea?'

'They're very good to take cuttings from, though they make a different kind of new growth from the hibiscus. This year's growth goes right back virtually down to the bottom of the plant, so you can't really take that as a cutting. Just cut off a suitable bit from the end of a growth, but make sure it's a non-flowering shoot.'

'Why is that important?'

'Well, you don't want the cutting putting all its energies into a flower that it can't really support at this stage. It needs to put everything into making new roots. Good roots mean a good plant.'

'Can I take lots of hydrangea cuttings?'

'Yes, provided the plant's got the right sort of material. With a lot of shrubs, thin cuttings root better than the thick, lush stems, so it's a good idea to have a few thin ones as well, then you're covered both ways.'

'How about purple berberis? Can I take cuttings from that?'

'With berberis, you tend to get two kinds of growth: very long, thin shoots and shorter shoots. The shorter ones are this year's growth, growing out of last year's. These will root much better than the long, thin sort. I shall take off a whole branch and divide it up later into cuttings. Do you fancy some rose cuttings?'

'I didn't know you could do rose cuttings.'

'Oh, yes. The nurseries always graft them because it's more convenient, but in fact roses growing on their own roots are much easier to look after as they don't have any suckers growing from the rootstock. It's just like taking any other kind of cuttings in mid-summer. A non-flowering shoot will do, and it doesn't even matter about mildew at the top, because that'll come off later.

'You can also take cuttings from plants such as hebe, philadelphus, forsythia, viburnum and weigela. In fact, it's well worth having a go with any shrub you'd like more of! The important thing is to take plenty of cuttings in case some fail.'

'What will I need for rooting the cuttings?'

'Some large pots, because you need to have enough depth to get the cuttings in, and some of them might be relatively long. Ordinary seed-sowing compost is fine to root cuttings in. Don't firm compost down while you're putting cuttings in, because you can end up with the

Right: *Hydrangea macrophylla* 'Blue Wave' is easily propagated from cuttings.

cutting being smothered in compost. It's better to firm the compost down first and then use a pencil or something similar to make a hole. Be careful not to make the hole too long for the cutting otherwise you might create an air pocket, which can lead ultimately to the cutting rotting.

'To prepare the cutting, tear away the lower leaves and take out any very soft growth from the top of the shoot, because that's likely to go rotten. If it does, it'll rot back and kill the cutting. The last thing to do is just trim off the cutting neatly at the bottom, underneath a leaf joint, and for that you'll need a sharp knife. So you end up with just a tiny little bit of the old wood, and it's ready to go in the pot.'

Trimming a cutting just below a leaf joint.

'No rooting powder?'

'It's a matter of personal taste. I find a lot of cuttings root terribly easily without it. However, cuttings tend to want to rot at the best of times, so do everything you can to stop them doing it – and that includes using rooting powder, because as well as the hormone it's usually got a fungicide in it. So it's not a bad idea to use it with thicker, softer shoots, as they are sappier and more prone to rotting.'

'What happens once I've got a pot full of cuttings?'

'Put three split canes in the edge of the pot and slip a large plastic bag loosely over it to keep a nice, humid environment around the cuttings. That stops them losing water vapour through the leaves until they've rooted.

When they do start rooting – after about six or eight weeks – they'll want a little bit of ventilation, so then you should make a few holes in the bag.

'John, you're lucky enough to have a greenhouse, but in fact you could do cuttings in a small way in a pot on the windowsill, provided it is shady. Any spare space outside, in the vegetable plot or in the flower garden, is ideal, too – particularly for you, when you've got a lot of cuttings to take to fill up that big new border!

'All you need is any reasonably well-prepared bit of soil that's fairly well drained. You could fork in a little bit of grit or peat if your soil is less than perfect. Instead of the plastic bag, use a cloche to cover the cuttings – ideally one with opaque plastic, because cuttings don't like a lot of sun. Just push the cuttings into the soil about 1½–2 inches [4–5 cm] apart. Then they need water, and the cloche goes over the top, with a sheet of glass at either end to block off the ends. By next autumn they'll be ready to dig up and plant into your border.'

'Excellent!'

'And all for nothing!'

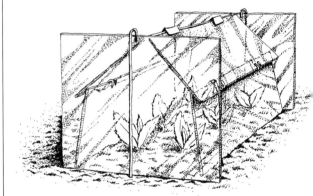

A basic cloche provides extra protection for cuttings.

Many climbing plants, such as honeysuckle, can be propagated by the simple method of layering. In the spring, take a young, low-growing shoot and trim off the leaves to provide a few inches of bare stem. Make a little cut on the underside of the shoot and sprinkle in some hormone rooting powder. Peg this piece of the shoot into the ground and cover it with 3 inches/7.5cm of earth. By the autumn it should have rooted and can be detached from the parent plant.

GROWING FROM SEED

One of the cheapest and most satisfying ways of filling the garden with colour is to grow hardy annuals and biennials from seed. You can sow the seeds directly into the ground in the position where they will eventually flower, but for best results it's worth making a decent seed bed first. Remove any weeds, fork over the soil (adding compost if it is poor) then firm it down and rake the surface so that no lumps remain.

You can either scatter the seeds all over the prepared area or sow them in rows about 1 inch/2.5 cm deep, using a line of string as a guide. Don't forget to label the seeds, then cover them over using the rake. Finally, water them in gently, using a fine rose on your watering can.

When the seeds have germinated they'll probably need thinning out. Keen gardeners usually do this in two stages, the first time leaving three times as many plants as will be needed. When these have grown on they can be thinned to the recommended planting distances, leaving the sturdiest plants to reach maturity.

Half-hardy annuals are more of a challenge and should be germinated in gentle warmth indoors, ideally using a small propagator. If you get really hooked it may be worth investing in a small greenhouse, which will provide ideal growing conditions for producing lots of plants from seed.

Making a drill prior to sowing some hardy varieties of seed.

However, if you want the fun of growing plants without the hassle of the initial germination phase, it may be worth buying pots of ready-grown seedlings or even young plants from garden centres or seed companies in the spring.

Apart from hardy annuals, my favourite plants for growing from seed are hardy perennials such as delphiniums and lupins. If these are sown in mid-summer, they'll be big enough by the following summer to produce a good display which will get bigger and better every year. Depending on the variety, a packet of seeds costing less than £1 will produce around 40 plants that will give years of pleasure. That's what I call value for money.

The colourful Russell hybrid lupins are easy to grow from seed.

Propagation questions and answers

I have a fuchsia cutting which I have rooted but, since potting, it is looking very ill. What is wrong?

Although the roots are developing well, the soil is probably too wet, so add some drainage to the bottom of the pot. Move it to a shady spot while it establishes itself, and nip out the top growth to make it bushy.

I put my geraniums in an unheated greenhouse over the winter period, but they don't survive. Can I take cuttings to grow on for next year's display?

An unheated greenhouse will not be a frost-free place so is not ideal for overwintering pelargoniums, or geraniums as they are more popularly known. Instead, put them in damp, but not wet, peat in a cardboard box, and store them in a frost-free place like a garage. If you have taken cuttings from pelargoniums in the late summer and kept them in the greenhouse under light shade to root, they can stay undisturbed in the greenhouse or conservatory as long as it is heated to keep the frost off. Cuttings will also root well in the spring, and can be taken from the old stock plants that have overwintered successfully and started growing again.

Why will my carrot seeds not germinate?

In hot, dry weather it is important to keep the seeds well watered. You could sow a new crop as late as the end of July and be pulling carrots at the end of September.

My delphinium, which used to produce six flower spikes a year, now seems to be looking weak with poor flowers. Why?

It sounds as though your plant is becoming tired. Lift the plant next year in the spring and divide it into smaller, new plants, using a knife if necessary. Each section should have a growth bud and roots. Then replant the pieces with a generous helping of bonemeal mixed into the soil. Water well, give them a good mulch, and you should get a fine display of flowers the following summer.

PRUNING

Gardening writer Matthew Biggs paid a visit to the Hatton fruit gardens at Horticultural Research International in Kent. Inspired by the gardens of Louis XIV at Versailles, they have been planted with apple and pear trees for the purpose of demonstrating pruning and training techniques to the amateur grower.

MATTHEW BIGGS:

'Your garden may not be as large and grand as the one at Versailles, but you can still grow fruit. Espaliers are perfect for smaller gardens. The compact shape, with tiers of horizontal branches coming out at right angles to a main vertical stem, means that they are easy to manage, the fruit is easy to pick, and they are very simple to prune. They never outgrow their space, either, because the main tree is grown on a dwarfing rootstock. Such an architecturally shaped tree will make a real feature in any garden – it will look highly ornamental in late summer covered in fruit, in the winter you will appreciate the real beauty of its shape, and it will look stunning in spring covered in blossom.

Apple blossom.

Apple trees can be extremely compact if grown on dwarf rooting stock.

'Another training method that's good for apples and pears is cordons. Planted about 2½ ft [75 cm] apart and at an angle of 45 degrees they don't take up much room, so you can afford to plant quite a lot in a small area and then you won't have any problems with pollinators.

'Both espaliers and cordons can be grown free-standing, against a wall or on a wire.

'Dwarf bushes, about 3 ft [90 cm] high, are another good shape. One problem is that the rootstock they're growing on is quite brittle, so they'll need permanent support from a stake. They also really need the soil around the base of the trunk to be kept clear of any other vegetation, as these small trees cannot cope with any competition from other plants. But for the fact that they can be a little bit fussy, they do make attractive little trees which are easy to manage, easy to harvest, and fruit-bearing from an early age.

'Pruning is something that puts many people off growing fruit trees, but if you follow a few common-sense rules, it really is very straightforward.

'Late summer to early autumn is the time to summer-prune trained fruit trees. Don't be tempted into tackling the pruning too early just because your tree looks untidy with all those long, wispy growths that have appeared through the summer. Pruned too early, trees will start growing again, and will then need a further tidying up.

'When it does come to the snip, those long, wispy, one-year-old growths are the ones that need atten-tion. Along the whole length of this new shoot will be dormant buds. It is impossible to know whether these are going to produce fruit or just more branches, but this is where pruning comes in — if you cut these stems hard back when the wood is starting to mature at the bottom they will then produce fruit buds.

'On existing side shoots, look for the cluster of leaves at the base of that year's growth. This cluster should be quite easy to spot, as the leaves will be noticeably closer together. Then simply count one leaf up the stem, above this cluster, and cut. Do this all over the whole bush or tree.

Prune at an angle away from the bud.

Above: Look for the cluster of leaves at the base of this year's growth.

Below: An apple tree trained as a handsome espalier.

'To make a first fruit cluster on a new side shoot, prune the long shoots coming from the main stem. Look for the basal group of leaves towards the base of these stems, count three leaves above this, and cut. Snipping these off will stimulate those buds below to be fruit buds and form the first cluster.

'Sharp secateurs are a must for good clean cuts. Blunt equipment will only result in ragged cuts, which could become infected with disease. Try to make your cuts at an angle sloping away from the bud. Rain water

will then run off away from the bud, leaving it dry. Don't prune too high above a bud, either, or the stem might die back.

'As well as producing fruit buds, summer pruning keeps the tree neat and in good health and allows the sunshine to ripen the wood and fruit.

'Once you have mastered the techniques for pruning cordons and espaliers, why not try something a little more daring and imaginative? At the Hatton fruit gardens they have all manner of weird and wonderful shapes, including an extraordinary boat and a crown. So get those secateurs out, and your fruit trees need never be boring again!'

As Matthew explains, regular pruning is necessary to ensure a good crop. While the principle is the same, the specific techniques vary considerably for other forms of fruit. For further details consult *The Fruit Garden Displayed*, with its easy-to-follow photographs. You can find details of the book in the reading list on page 137.

Pruning questions and answers

I have a large, healthy climbing rose on a north wall that will not flower, even though I prune it properly in the autumn.

You could be pruning a bit too early and perhaps not quite hard enough. As it is vigorous, prune it hard and tie in the laterals to encourage flowering buds to break along the stem. Alternatively, leave pruning for a whole year and see if it flowers then. When planting a rose, always choose the right one for the specific situation. Suitable climbers for a north-facing wall would be 'Zéphirine Drouhin', 'Gloire de Dijon', 'New Dawn', 'Golden Showers' and 'Madame Grégoire Staechelin'.

Why did my *Lavatera* die off after two years?

The tree mallow (*Lavatera olbia*) is generally short-lived, lasting only around four to five years. Hard winters can kill it off, too, as it is not particularly tough. Give it a sunny position and cut it back every spring to about 12 inches/30 cm from the ground, and this should keep it vigorous. It will repay you for all the trouble with an abundant display of open, colourful flowers in late summer. The bees and insects will thank you, too.

When should I prune my walnut tree?

It is best to prune this handsome tree when it is in full leaf – early August is ideal – but only do a little at a time. Small cuts will heal quickly. If your tree is large, it is wise to get in a professional tree surgeon who is a member of the Arboricultural Association.

How often should I prune my wisteria? It is getting out of control.

Unless it is given an annual prune to keep it in check, wisteria can gallop all over the wall, the guttering, and even the roof. This very popular plant prefers a position on a south- or south-west-facing wall where it will happily produce the characteristic bunches of lavender-blue flowers. Allow young plants to establish a framework of branches before starting to prune; on mature plants cut back long wispy sideshoots to six leaves in August. In February these should be cut back again to two leaf nodes (joints) to encourage flowering buds to develop. This is also a good time to thin out any overcrowded branches. Take out any extra shoots coming from the base of the main stem, as the ideal shape is a single stem opening up into a network of lateral branches.

I have a *Magnolia* × *soulangeana* that is approximately 30 years old. It has grown so large that it's now blocking the view from our house. Is it possible to prune this shrub without affecting its ability to flower?

Prune only after flowering, ideally in the autumn or early winter, and the magnolia will be fine. As your shrub sounds healthy and vigorous you should be able to prune it quite hard without affecting its flowering.

Why is my variegated ivy going green?

It is just reverting to its original form, and the green growth should simply be cut out.

My *Fremontodendron* 'California Glory' is outgrowing its space. Can I prune it?

This lovely evergreen plant with sunny yellow flowers simply needs its top removing to keep it under control. Take care, though – the plant has small brown hairs on the stem that can irritate the skin.

My eucalyptus tree was vandalized and now there is only a stump left. Will it recover?

Eucalyptus respond well to pruning, so cut it right down to the ground and it should start shooting again, especially if you feed and water it regularly. The best time to do this is spring or early summer, so that the new growth has time to toughen up before the colder weather sets in. If you leave it too late, the delicate young growth could be destroyed by frost.

Can I prune a rather large old smoke bush back into shape?

Cotinus coggyria responds well to pruning and can be cut down to the ground in winter. However, to minimize the shock to your elderly plant, cut half of it one winter and then do the rest the following year. This will encourage it to produce strong new growths and plenty of the 'smoke' for which this bush is renowned.

Magnolias can be pruned in the autumn if they grow too big.

HEDGES

Hedges provide colour, texture and shape for the garden. They're far prettier and certainly more versatile than fences – a hedge can be neatly formal or decoratively informal, depending on your needs.

One of the finest of all formal hedges is yew, but it takes six to ten years to establish. Considerably faster-growing is the Leyland cypress. The golden form (× *Cupressocyparis* 'Castlewellan') is showier, but both will need clipping twice a year to keep them under control and stop them becoming very tall and wide.

Box is the ideal evergreen for neat, low hedges – especially *Buxus sempervirens* 'Suffruticosa', which can happily be maintained at just 12 inches/30 cm high. Planting a hedge can be expensive, so buy young plants from a specialist nursery to save a fortune on garden-centre prices. Alternatively, buy a few pots of large plants like *Escallonia*, *Viburnum tinus* or *Rosa rugosa* and take lots of cuttings.

Regular trimming is essential to keep a formal hedge looking good. To deflect strong winds and snow, it should ideally be narrower at the top than the bottom, because the base will support sloping sides far more effectively. Wind will flow over a tapered hedge rather than push against it, and snow has a smaller area to settle on.

To achieve a level top to your hedge, stretch a string tightly between two upright posts or stout canes. Position the string at the height you want to cut the hedge and then use it as a guide.

PLANT LIST

Ten best hedge plants

(Evergreen except where stated)

Buxus sempervirens (box): Small-leaved and slow-growing, ideal for low hedging and knot gardens.

Fagus sylvatica (beech): Fast-growing. Deciduous, but holds its leaves through winter.

Griselinia littoralis: Shining, leathery leaves. Useful for seaside gardens in milder districts.

Ilex (holly): A wide range of leaf type and colour; makes a dense, impenetrable screen.

Lavandula (lavender): The classic cottage-garden hedge. Short-lived but easily increased from cuttings.

Ligustrum (privet): A reliable old favourite. The golden-leaved form is good.

Lonicera nitida 'Baggesen's Gold': Tiny-leaved, fast-growing. Great for sculpted hedges and topiary.

Rosa rugosa: For an exuberant rose hedge. Fragrant flowers, large hips and good disease resistance. Deciduous.

Rosmarinus (rosemary): An excellent informal hedge. Blue flowers and aromatic grey-green leaves.

Taxus baccata (yew): The aristocrat of hedges, with a sumptuous dark green colour. Pamper when young.

THE FLOWER-ARRANGER'S GARDEN

As well as appreciating the flowers in your garden, why not grow some to enjoy in the house as well? There are many plants that will produce enough flowers for cutting while still leaving plenty in your border. In Wiltshire, I met Peggy Parsons, one of the flower-arrangers for Salisbury Cathedral. Such a wonderful building demands floral displays of equal beauty, and Peggy and a team of arrangers keep the cathedral decked in flowers all year round.

Peggy and her neighbour, Margaret Browne, are responsible for providing the arrangers with all their flowers and foliage, and the two had some handy tips.

A colourful combination of garden and florists' flowers.

Rich pickings for the flower-arranger.

● Picking your own flowers is much more fun than buying them and it allows you to choose exactly the right kind of blooms for an arrangement. It'll also save you a small fortune on florists' bills.

● Choose your plants with care so that you have a variety to cut for as long a season as possible. You don't want lots of flowers in the spring and then none at all in the summer.

● Height is important, particularly if you're doing an arrangement in a church. Large-scale buildings demand large-scale floral displays.

● While you're at it, grow a selection of shrubs that will supply you with foliage to accompany your flowers. You will get far more variety in your garden than a florist would ever be able to supply you with. Plant a mixture of deciduous and evergreen shrubs and you will then be able to pick foliage all year round. Choose plants that will give you a good combination of texture, shape and colour and will grow quite vigorously to give you lots to cut. Don't forget that berries can be very useful in those dark winter months, especially around Christmas, as can colourful stems. The

vibrant red stems of *Cornus alba* (dogwood) can't fail to brighten up a winter arrangement.

● When planning a border for cut flowers and foliage, try to create a basic framework of shrubs surrounded by perennials and annuals. This will create a useful border packed with lots of cutting material, while still looking attractive.

● Try to be a little imaginative when cutting flowers and leaves. A yellowing *Fatsia* leaf may be exactly the right colour for an arrangement, and a twisted stem might be just what you need to add a bit of flair.

● When it comes to cutting, avoid the heat of the midday sun as plants can quickly wilt. It is far better to cut what you need in the cool of the evening or early morning.

● All flowers and foliage must be conditioned after they have been cut. This involves soaking the stems in buckets of water for a few hours, or preferably overnight, so that they will last longer in an arrangement. Many plants will collapse and wilt very quickly if they are not conditioned. Thick, woody stems of shrubs should be split vertically to allow them to take up water. Seal the stems of flowers that leak sticky sap, like *Euphorbia*, by plunging the ends into boiling water for a few seconds.

You can make floral arrangements in all manner of containers, using florist's foam or chicken wire to hold foliage and flowers in place. For a simple arrangement, just use a pretty jug filled with your favourites from the garden and you can't go wrong.

Keep the water topped up daily to keep the display fresh. Adding a small sachet of cut-flower food or a teaspoon of sugar to the water at the outset will provide the flowers with sustenance to keep them going.

If you want the arrangement to last as long as possible, condition your flowers and foliage well, remember to top up the water, keep in as cool a room as possible, and avoid direct sunlight.

PLANT LISTS

As nominated by Peggy Parsons.

Deciduous foliage

Berberis thunbergii f. *atropurpurea* (purple-leaf barberry): Dense, arching branches of reddish-purple foliage that turns bright red in autumn. Pale yellow flowers in mid-spring, followed by small red fruits. Watch out for the lethal thorns.

Ligustrum ovalifolium 'Argenteum' (silver privet): A vigorous, semi-evergreen, upright shrub with glossy mid-green oval leaves edged with silvery-white.

Ligustrum ovalifolium 'Aureum' (golden privet): Similar to silver privet but with leaves edged in bright yellow.

Physocarpus opulifolius (nine bark): Dense, arching stems with peeling bark. Broad, oval, toothed leaves with tiny pink-tinged white flowers in early summer.

Rosa glauca (syn. *R. rubrifolia*): This lovely rose is grown more for its beautiful grey-purple leaves than for its pink dog-rose flowers. Red hips in autumn.

Evergreen foliage

Aucuba japonica 'Crotonifolia' (spotted laurel): Masses of large, glossy green leaves, heavily mottled with yellow. A very tough, easy-to-grow plant. It sometimes produces small purple flowers in mid-spring, followed by red berries.

Fatsia japonica: Large, palmate, handsome mid-green leaves are plentiful on this splendid plant. It is more commonly grown as a houseplant, but will grow equally well in sheltered conditions in the garden.

Mahonia aquifolium (mountain grape): A smaller, more open-leaved relative of *M. japonica*. The glossy, bright green leaves often turn purple in winter. Blue-black berries form after the yellow flowers are over.

Mahonia japonica: An upright plant with glossy, spiny leaves. Long sprays of fragrant yellow flowers from late autumn to spring, then purple-blue fruits.

Rhamnus alaternus 'Argenteovariegatus' (Italian buckthorn): Oval, leathery, glossy grey leaves margined in creamy-white. Small yellow flowers in mid-summer turn into red then black fruits.

Flowers

There is an enormous range to recommend, but the following suggestions are what Peggy believes to be the basics for every flower-arranger.

Agapanthus Headbourne hybrids: Clump-forming perennials with large clusters of blue, trumpet-shaped flowers, strap-like foliage and tall stems.

Alchemilla mollis (lady's mantle): A pretty perennial with attractive, crinkly-edged, mid-green leaves. Lots of lime-green flowers are produced in summer.

Alstroemeria hybrids: Summer-flowering perennials with multi-coloured showy flowers held in clusters on long stems. The flowers are produced in quite large numbers and last very well when cut.

Lathyrus odoratus (sweet pea): Surely everyone's favourite annual. Climbing tendrils produce pretty, scented flowers in a multitude of colours.

Sedum spectabile 'Autumn Joy': A perennial with plate-like flower heads made up of many tiny purple flowers. Grey succulent-like foliage. Good for flowers late in the year.

LAWNS

The lawn is one of the most important features in the garden. In winter, it's probably the only substantial patch of green around, and in summer it acts as a foil to everything else. In essence, it sets the tone of the garden, so it's important to keep it looking neat.

However, a lawn of bowling-green perfection will require a great deal of hard labour, so if you want to minimize your workload, forget it. Just concentrate on regular mowing (at no lower than 1 inch/2.5 cm), keep the edges trimmed, and you'll have a perfectly acceptable lawn.

There are a few other points worth knowing:

Only bother with feeding in the autumn. Use a proper autumn/winter feed, and it'll build up the strength of the lawn in time for next year's pounding feet. (However, if the lawn looks particularly poor it would benefit from a spring feed as well.)

Don't fret about weeds as long as they're not taking over. Many people actually enjoy daisies in the lawn, and clover is now considered positively beneficial, partly because it stays green in time of drought. The occasional big weed – like a dandelion – can be dug out or destroyed using a spot of weedkiller.

If the lawn is too mossy, there's usually a problem with poor drainage, acid soil or shade. For long-term control, try to tackle the underlying cause. To improve drainage, for instance, spike the lawn using a garden fork or, even better, a hired hollow tine aerator. Then topdress using a 50:50 mixture of horticultural sand and loamy soil.

If the lawn is bumpy, lift up the offending turf and scrape away some soil on the ridge. Hollows, on the other hand, can be filled with compost, 1 inch/2.5 cm at a time. Let the grass grow through before adding more.

Lawn questions and answers

How do I get rid of speedwell from my lawn?

This pretty weed can be a problem if not controlled. Hand-weeding is possible if only a few plants are present, otherwise use a problem-lawn weedkiller. Apply it in spring for maximum success.

My lawn is meadow grass. I would prefer finer grass, so should I returf it all?

Cultivated turf is usually much finer than meadow grass, but if you have young children, why not leave the lawn as it is? Meadow grass is very hardwearing. Once the children have stopped using the lawn as a football pitch, you can change it for finer grass!

How do I care for a newly seeded lawn?

The best time to sow is in the autumn, although spring is not out of the question. Prepare the soil well and feed it. Clear away any weeds and rake the surface to get a fine, level tilth. Sort out any drainage problems in advance – if water stands for 24 hours you've got a drainage problem, and you'll need to get to work with a fork or an aerator.

Once you've sown the seeds, you may need to keep the birds off! The first mowing can take place when the grass is 2½ inches/6 cm high. If it's only a small area, it might be easier to use shears. Don't worry when weeds appear, as these will go when you start regular mowing. Persistent weeds, like plantains, can be dug out later, or treated with a spot weeder.

I've just laid some turves, and big cracks have appeared between each of the pieces. What can I do about this?

Turf sometimes shrinks. This usually happens in dry weather, especially if the turves weren't laid close enough together in the first place.

To repair the cracks, water the lawn well and wait for the turves to expand back to their original size. Then brush in a mixture of either good garden soil or a top dressing (soil, washed sand and peat, which you can buy ready-mixed at a garden centre, although it may be cheaper to mix your own). Kept well-watered, the grass will grow into the fresh soil and the cracks will soon disappear.

A good-looking lawn need not be hard work.

A DOWN-TO-EARTH GUIDE TO ENJOYABLE GARDENING

GARDENS TO VISIT

One of the most enjoyable ways of improving your garden is to go garden visiting. Even in the grandest stately gardens you'll find new plants and plant associations that you might well be tempted to try out at home.

However, it's the smaller, privately owned gardens that I love the most. These are featured in *Gardens of England and Wales* (affectionately nicknamed *The Yellow Book*), which is published annually. Many of them are gems, usually opening in aid of charity just once or twice a year when they are at their peak. They provide the opportunity for a wonderful afternoon outing – especially if there's a home-made tea available. It's thirsty work, garden visiting!

In addition to the thousands of excellent gardens featured in *The Yellow Book* (and the equivalent publications for Scotland and Northern Ireland), I can particularly recommend:

Barnsley House, near Cirencester, Gloucestershire.
Tel. 0285 74281.
Created by Rosemary Verey, this is one of the most exciting gardens I've ever visited. It is crammed full of good design ideas, the planting is inspired and the ornamental kitchen garden is mouthwatering.

Biddulph Grange, Biddulph, Stoke-on-Trent, Staffordshire.
Tel. 0782 517999.
A Victorian extravaganza, now lovingly restored by the National Trust. It is something of a world tour, with eccentric touches – to reach the Chinese garden, for instance, you enter a topiary-bedecked Egyptian doorway and emerge through a half-timbered Cheshire cottage. Terrific fun, and marvellous plants and plantings.

Bodnant Gardens, Tal-Y-Cafn, Colwyn Bay, Gwynedd.
Tel. 0492 650460.
One of the finest National Trust gardens in the country, in a beautiful setting above the River Conway overlooking Snowdonia. Spring is a wonderful time in this garden, with many rhododendrons, camellias and magnolias in flower. Alternatively, try to visit in May when the famous Laburnum Arch is in full flower – it's a stunning sight.

Chatsworth, Bakewell, Derbyshire.
Tel. 0246 582204.
A superb 100-acre/47-hectare garden containing various fashions from its 300-year development, including a woodland garden, colour-themed borders, a rose garden and an old conservatory garden. The stepped waterfall is perfect for cooling the feet on a hot summer's day. One tip – don't try to go round the gardens and house in one day, as both have so much in them that they deserve a day set aside for each.

Denmans, Fontwell, near Arundel, Sussex.
Tel. 0243 542808.
A wonderful garden started by Mrs Robinson in 1946 and continued by the leading landscape designer John Brookes. It is famous for its imaginative and extravagant plantings, in which plants and materials are combined to provide form, colour and texture. There's a good collection of tender plants as well.

Great Dixter, Northiam, Rye, East Sussex.
Tel. 0797 43160.
The garden of Christopher Lloyd, one of the most important gardeners (and garden writers) of this century. The beautiful fifteenth-century house is surrounded by wonderful plantings, including the famous long border, the wildflower meadow and the new subtropical garden. A must.

Inverewe Gardens, Poolewe, Ross and Cromarty.
Tel. 044 586 200.
Gardens of great beauty, established on a virtually soilless rocky outcrop overlooking Loch Ewe. Thanks to a shelter belt of pines and firs and the warming waters of the Gulf Stream, many rare and delicate plants can be grown here, including palms and tree ferns. They are especially good at rhododendron time, but worth a visit every day of the year.

Levens Hall, Kendal, Cumbria.
Tel. 05395 60321.
If you're a fan of topiary, this is the garden for you. It has hardly changed since it was designed in the seventeenth century and contains huge clipped yew trees of all shapes, in beds of seasonal bedding surrounded by box hedging.

Powis Castle, Welshpool, Powys.
Tel. 0938 554336.
A grand historic garden set around a thirteenth-century castle. The stunning series of steep terraces are defined by massive clipped hedges and packed with colourful plantings. There are plenty of ideas to pick up, especially from their glorious and innovative planted containers.

Sissinghurst Castle, near Cranbrook, Kent.
Tel. 0580 712850.
One of the most admired English gardens in the world. For design, plant associations and sheer atmosphere it's hard to beat. The only aggravation is that it's so popular that the National Trust has to limit the number of visitors – so check in advance.

Wisley Gardens, near Ripley, Woking, Surrey.
Tel. 0483 224234.
A perfectionist display of gardening at its best – as you'd expect, for it's the home of the Royal Horticultural Society. There's everything from model fruit gardens to alpine houses, grand herbaceous borders and a superb rock garden. An excellent day out, but with one minor criticism – the food, though good, is very pricey.

For even more good gardens, see Patrick Taylor's *The Gardener's Guide to Britain*, published by Pavilion Books.

RECOMMENDED BOOKS

Inevitably, in this book I have only been able to touch the surface of a few gardening topics, so I have selected some appropriate titles for those who would like to read more. Although it is difficult to pick out just a few good books, these are personal favourites:

Bedding Plants by Graham Rice, RHS/Cassell, £3.95.

Carnivorous Plants by Adrian Slack, A & C Black, £12.95.

Christopher Lloyd's Flower Garden by Christopher Lloyd, Dorling Kindersley, £15.99.

The Complete Book of Herbs by Lesley Bremness, Dorling Kindersley, £15.99.

The Complete Manual of Organic Gardening by Basil Caplin, Headline, £25.00.

The Complete Small Garden by Graham Rice, Macmillan, £9.99.

The Conservatory Gardener by Anne Swithinbank, Frances Lincoln, £20.00.

Creative Container Gardening by Kathleen Brown and Effie Romain, Mermaid Books, £12.99.

The Flower Arranger's Garden by Rosemary Verey, Conran Octopus, £9.99.

The Fruit Garden Displayed (RHS) by Harry Baker, Cassell, £10.99.

The Fruit and Vegetable Clinic by Pippa Greenwood, Ward Lock, £5.99.

Gardens of England and Wales 1994. Available from all good bookshops and some garden centres, £3.00, or £3.75 inc. p & p from the National Gardens Scheme, Hatchlands Park, East Clandon, Guildford, Surrey GU4 7RT.

The Houseplant Clinic by Pippa Greenwood, Ward Lock, £5.99.

How to Make a Wildlife Garden by Chris Baines, Hamish Hamilton, £9.99.

John Brookes' Garden Design Book by John Brookes, Dorling Kindersley, £22.50.

Magic Muck: The Complete Guide to Compost by Lady Muck, Pavilion Books, £9.99.

Making the Most of Clematis by Raymond Evison, Burrall and Floraprint, £5.95.

Oriental Vegetables by Joy Larkcom, John Murray, £16.95.

The PBI 'Expert' range: subjects include rock and water gardens, garden DIY, houseplants, roses, lawns, trees and shrubs, flowers, vegetables and fruit. Dr D. G. Hessayon, Pan Britannica Industries Publications, £4.50

Perennials (Volumes 1 & 2) by Roger Phillips and Martyn Rix, Pan Books, £13.99 each.

The RHS Gardeners' Encylopedia of Plants and Flowers, ed Christopher Brickell, Dorling Kindersley, £29.95.

Right Plant, Right Place by Nicola Ferguson, Pan Books, £12.99.

Roses by Roger Phillips and Martyn Rix, Pan Books, £12.99.

The Vegetable Garden Displayed (RHS) by Joy Larkcom, Batsford, £10.95.

Vegetables by Roger Phillips and Martyn Rix, Pan Books, £17.50.

Vegetables for Small Gardens by Joy Larkcom, Faber & Faber, £4.99.

The Well Tempered Garden by Christopher Lloyd, Penguin, £14.99.

GLOSSARY OF COMMON GARDENING TERMS

Annual: A plant that germinates, flowers, seeds and dies within one growing season, e.g. nasturtium.

Bare-root: Applied to plants such as roses, hedging plants and trees which are lifted from the ground and sold with the roots bare of soil.

Biennial: A plant which produces flowers in the second year after germination and then sets seed and dies, e.g. foxgloves, sweet william.

Blanch: To exclude light from a portion of a vegetable in order to keep it tender, as with celery and leeks.

Blind: Of a plant which fails to produce flowers – very common in daffodils when not planted deeply enough.

Bolting: Of a leafy vegetable, e.g. spinach, which produces flowers and seed prematurely and is no further use as a leaf crop.

Bract: A modified leaf often resembling a petal, e.g. the showy red bracts of poinsettias.

Catch crop: A quick-growing crop planted in the same ground as one which is slower to spread and mature, e.g. radish sown with lettuce, to maximize use of ground.

Cloche: A portable plastic or glass cover to protect crops from cold and extend the growing season.

Cold frame: A brick, wood or glazed box with a glass lid, used to protect plants from excessive cold outdoors.

Cordon: A method of training a tree (usually an apple) by restricting it to one main stem which is grown at an angle of 45 degrees to maximize fruit yield. It is usually used where space is at a premium.

Crocks: Broken pieces of clay pot used at the bottom of plant containers to prevent the compost from blocking the drainage hole.

Crown: In a tree, the canopy of leaves and branches. In a herbaceous plant, the base from which new shoots emerge.

Cuttings: Portions of stem, leaf or root that are potted up to form new

plants. Irishman's cuttings are portions of stem with a few roots attached.

Damping down: Wetting greenhouse floors to increase humidity, done especially in very hot weather. Any of the cucumber family will appreciate this.

Dead-heading: Removing flowers regularly to prevent the plant's energy from going into seed production instead of further flowers.

Division: Increasing a stock of clump-forming plants by lifting and dividing them into smaller portions.

Drifts: Plants placed so that they look as though they have arisen naturally. Especially good for daffodils in grass.

Drill: A furrow in well-prepared soil into which seeds are sown.

Earthing up: Mounding earth round plants, e.g. potatoes, celery or leeks.

Ericaceous: Referring to plants, those that prefer an acid (peaty) soil, such as rhododendrons. Also referring to composts, those that are specially formulated for such plants.

Espalier: A trained tree which has a main stem and three or more tiers of horizontal branches on either side. Usually used for fruit, especially against a wall.

Force: To encourage plants to flower or fruit sooner than they would naturally, usually by applying heat.

Fungicide: Any proprietary substance that kills fungi, such as those responsible for black spot and rust.

Germination: The point at which a seed starts into growth.

Graft: The point at which two plants are artificially joined. Most roses and fruit trees, for instance, are grafted onto special rootstocks. Some ornamental trees have weeping heads grafted onto clear stems, e.g. the Kilmarnock willow.

Growing point: The point from which most growth is made – i.e. leading stems and sideshoots rather than subsidiary growths.

Half hardy: Plants which will be killed by frosts, e.g. bedding fuchsias.

Hardy: A plant that can be grown outdoors year-round without any protection.

Heel: The small strip of wood or bark at the base of a cutting when it is

pulled from a main stem.

Herbaceous: A non-woody plant that dies back to the crown over winter.

Insecticide: Any proprietary substance that kills insects such as greenfly and blackfly.

Laterals: Any side growths from a main stem or branch.

Layering: Pinning a shoot to the ground while still attached to the parent plant. The resultant rooted plant can be severed and grown on. This often occurs naturally.

Leader: The main central stem of a tree or shrub.

Microclimate: A climate that occurs in a very small area, e.g. the north and south sides of a wall.

Mulch: A layer of material such as chipped bark, compost or polythene, used to suppress weeds and retain moisture.

Naturalizing: Growing plants to look as if they are in the wild, e.g. crocuses or daffodils in lawns, bluebells under trees.

Offset: A young plant, usually produced from the base of the parent plant, that can be severed and grown on.

Organic matter: Any plant material, e.g. composted straw, kitchen waste, shredded bark or prunings, that can be added to the soil to improve its consistency and help increase its fertility.

Over-winter: To keep a plant in special conditions (usually protected from frost) during the winter months.

Palmate: Broad, fingered leaves, such as those of *Fatsia japonica*.

Perennial: Technically, any plant with a lifespan of more than three years. Most perennials will far exceed this.

Pinch out: To take out the tender growing tip of a plant to encourage the formation of side shoots. This will create a bushier shape, and more blooms on flowering plants such as sweet peas.

Pollination: The transfer of pollen from a male to a female flower in order for it to become fertile and produce fruit.

Potting on: Transferring a plant to a larger pot.

Potting up: Transferring seedlings or small plants into individual pots.

Pricking out: Gently teasing crowded seedlings from pots and transferring them to seed trays or small individual pots.

Propagation: Raising more plants from existing stock by sowing seeds, taking cuttings, layering etc.

Propagator: A heated or unheated box with a clear lid for raising seedlings and cuttings.

Rootstock: The root system of one plant which is grafted onto the top growth of another of the same species. Roses are often grown on wild rose rootstocks to create a more vigorous root system. Dwarfing rootstocks are used on fruit trees to restrict their size.

Root-wrapped: Bare-root plants supplied in protective wrapping.

Runner: A long stem on which young plants form and root where they touch the earth.

Self-seed: The ability of a plant to shed seeds that germinate around it without the provision of any special conditions. Forget-me-not is a good example of a self-seeder.

Slow-release fertilizer: Any fertilizer that releases nutrients over a long period. Most organic fertilizers act this way, and some chemical ones (especially those for containers) have been formulated to do the same.

Specimen plant: One that is placed as a focal point, often where it can be viewed from all angles.

Spit: A spade's depth (blade only!).

Sport: A shoot that produces leaves or flowers which differ from those of the parent plant.

Spur: A short branch that bears flowers (usually applied to fruit trees).

Standard: Of trees, those that have a good length of clear stem below the branches. Half standards branch from lower down the stem, at around 3 ft/ 90 cm. A standard shrub is one that has been specially trained on a single clear stem.

Sucker: Vigorous stems arising from the rootstocks of grafted plants. Most common on roses when not planted at the correct depth.

Syn.: Short for 'synonymous' and used

where a plant has two commonly used names, e.g. the ivy *Hedera colchica* 'Sulphur Heart', syn. 'Paddy's Pride'.

Systemic: A fungicide or pesticide that is absorbed into a plant, giving longer-lasting protection than contact sprays, which remain on leaf and stem surfaces.

Tender: Any plant that is susceptible to frost.

Thinning: Removing plant material, e.g. thinning seedlings to prevent overcrowding, thinning grapes for better development.

Tilth: The crumbly surface texture of well-cultivated soil.

Trace elements: Also known as micronutrients, these are small quantities of chemical elements that are essential to plant growth.

Trench: A strip of deeply dug soil, usually with compost added e.g. for sweet peas and runner beans.

RECOMMENDED MAIL ORDER SUPPLIERS

Arne Herbs,
Limeburn Nurseries,
Limeburn Hill,
Chew Magna,
Avon BS18 8QW.
Tel. 0275 333399.
Herbs, plus wild and cottage flowers.

The Beth Chatto Gardens Ltd,
Elmstead Market,
Colchester,
Essex CO7 7DB.
Tel. 0206 822007.
Unusual herbaceous plants.

Bressingham Gardens Mail Order,
Bressingham,
Diss,
Norfolk IP22 2AB.
Tel. 0379 88 464.
Wide range of hardy ornamental plants.

Broadleigh Gardens,
Bishops Hull,
Taunton,
Somerset TA4 1AE.
Tel. 0823 286231.
Bulbs, including dwarf and unusual.

Buckingham Nurseries,
14 Tingewick Road,
Buckingham,
Bucks MK18 4AE.
Tel. 0280 815491.
Bare root and container hedging.

Burncoose & South Down Nurseries,
Gwennap,
Redruth,
Cornwall TR16 6BJ.
Tel. 0209 861112.
Trees, shrubs and herbaceous plants.

Chase Organics Ltd,
Coombelands House,
Addlestone,
Weybridge,
Surrey KT15 1HY.
Tel. 0932 820958.
Organic seeds and sundries.

Chiltern Seeds,
Bortree Stile,
Ulverston,
Cumbria LA12 7PB.
Tel. 0229 581137.
Almost 4,000 seed varieties, many of them rare.

David Austin Roses Ltd,
Bowling Green Lane,
Albrighton,
Wolverhampton,
West Midlands WV7 3HB.
Tel. 0902 373931.
A wide selection of roses, including old varieties.

Deacon's Nursery,
Moorview,
Godshill,
Isle of Wight PO38 3HW.
Tel. 0983 840750.
A comprehensive range of top fruit.

P. de Jager and Sons Ltd,
Staplehurst Road,
Marden,
Kent TN12 9BP.
Tel. 0622 831235.
One of the widest ranges of bulbs available.

Global Orange Groves,
PO Box 644,
Poole,
Dorset BH17 9YB.
Tel. 0202 691699.
Citrus trees and fertilizer.

Hopleys Plants Ltd,
High Street,
Much Hadham,
Herts SG10 6BU.
Tel. 0279 84 2509.
Shrubs and perennials.

Jacques Amand Ltd,
The Nurseries,
145 Clamp Hill,
Stanmore,
Middlesex HA7 3JS.
Tel. 081 954 8138.
Bulbs, including rare and unusual species.

Ken Muir,
Honeypot Farm,
Rectory Road,
Weeley Heath,
Clacton-on-Sea,
Essex CO16 9BJ.
Tel. 0255 830181.
A full range of soft fruit.

**Kingsfield Conservation
Nursery**,
Broadenham Lane,
Winsham,
Chard,
Somerset TA20 4JF.
Tel. 0460 30070.
Native trees, shrubs and flowers.

S. E. Marshall & Co Ltd,
Wisbech,
Cambs PE13 12RF.
Tel. 0945 588235.
Vegetable seed specialists.

Marston Exotics,
Brampton Lane,
Madley,
Herefordshire HR2 9LX.
Tel. 0981 251140.
**Specialize in insect-catching
plants.**

Reads Nursery,
Hales Hall,
Loddon,
Norfolk NR14 6QW.
Tel. 0508 548 395.
Conservatory plant specialists.

Scotts Nurseries (Merriott) Ltd,
Merriot,
Somerset TA16 5PL.
Tel. 0460 72306.
**An extremely wide general
range of plants.**

Stapeley Water Gardens Ltd,
London Road,
Stapeley,
Nantwich,
Cheshire CW5 7LH.
Tel. 0270 623 868.
**Water garden plants and
products.**

Suffolk Herbs,
Monks Farm,
Pantlings Lane,
Kelvedon,
Essex CO5 9PG.
Tel. 0376 572456.
**Herb, vegetable and wildflower
seeds and sundries.**

Thompson & Morgan,
London Road,
Ipswich,
Suffolk IP2 0BA.
Tel. 0473 688821.
**An extensive general range of
seeds.**

Trehane Camellia Nursery,
Stapehill Road,
Hampreston,
Wimborne,
Dorset BH21 7NE.
Tel. 0202 873490.
Camellias and ericaceous plants.

The Valley Clematis Nursery,
Willingham Road,
Hainton,
Lincs LN3 6LN.
Tel. 0507 313398.
A wide range of clematis.

ACKNOWLEDGEMENTS

A great team has been involved in the development of this book. Thank you to Mary McAnally of Meridian Television, who commissioned the television series, and to the brilliant production team, led by Carol Haslam and John Thornicroft at Hawkshead, who made it so much fun. The book wouldn't have appeared at all were it not for the guidance of Frances Whitaker and the cheerful typing of Lisa O'Gorman and Rebecca Kelly. Finally, I owe a great debt to Carolyn Hutchinson, who has been a marvellous source of help and inspiration.

INDEX

Page references in *italic* refer to illustrations, and * denotes a list of plants.

GRASS ROOTS

A DOWN-TO-EARTH GUIDE TO ENJOYABLE GARDENING

PICTURE CREDITS

The publishers are grateful to the following for permission to reproduce illustrations:

Andrew Anderson: pp. 2, 17, 43, 118 and line drawings on pp. 16, 19, 20, 22, 23, 28, 29, 35, 44, 45, 49, 54, 55, 60, 62, 65, 68, 71, 72, 74, 83, 86, 91, 94, 99, 102, 110, 116, 117, 122, 125, 127
Eric Crichton: pp. 21, 39, 59, 64, 69, 74, 82 (top)
Jerry Harpur: pp. 78, 88–9
Hawkshead Ltd: pp. 1, 6, 10–11, 25, 27, 28, 29, 50, 57, 58 (right), 61, 70 (both), 92, 95, 97, 103 (all), 108, 109, 121, 126, 127, 131, 132, 135
Richard Jackson: pp. 73, 77, 85, 96, 129
Andrew Lawson: pp. 30, 54, 58 (left), 66, 72
Clive Nichols: pp. 12, 14–16 (designer: Pam Lewis)
Photos Horticultural: pp. 8, 22, 32, 36, 37, 38, 40 (both), 44, 47, 48, 53, 56, 63, 75, 76, 81, 82 (bottom), 87, 91, 98, 100, 104, 107, 110, 111, 112, 113, 114, 115, 123, 124